George Whitefield

George Whitefield

God's Anointed Servant in the Great Revival of the Eighteenth Century

Arnold A. Dallimore

CROSSWAY BOOKS • WESTCHESTER, ILLINOIS
A DIVISION OF GOOD NEWS PUBLISHERS

George Whitefield: God's Anointed Servant in the Great Revival of the Eighteenth Century. Adapted, rewritten and abridged from the two-volume work published previously under the title: *George Whitefield: The Life and Times of the Great Evangelist of the Eighteen-Century Revival.*

Copyright © 1990 by Arnold A. Dallimore.

Published by Crossway Books, a division of
Good News Publishers, Westchester, Illinois 60154.

First printing, 1990

Printed in the United States of America

Library of Congress Catalog Card Number 89-81258

ISBN 0-89107-553-4

For the preaching of the cross is to them that perish foolishness; but unto us which are saved it is the power of God.

For after that in the wisdom of God the world by wisdom knew not God, it pleased God by the foolishness of preaching to save them that believe.

And I, brethren, when I came to you, came not with excellency of speech or wisdom, declaring unto you the testimony of God.

For I determined not to know any thing among you, save Jesus Christ, and him crucified.

And I was with you in weakness, and in fear, and in much trembling.

And my speech and my preaching was not with enticing words of man's wisdom, but in demonstration of the Spirit and of power:

That your faith should not stand in the wisdom of man, but in the power of God.

The Apostle Paul
1 Corinthians 1 and 2

Table of Contents

If ever philanthropy burned in the human heart with pure and intense flame, embracing the whole family of man in the spirit of universal charity, it was in the heart of George Whitefield. 'He loved the world that hated him.' He had no preferences but in favour of the ignorant, the miserable and the poor. In their cause he shrank from no privation, and declined neither insult nor hostility. To such wrongs he opposed the weapons of an all-enduring meekness and a love which would not be repulsed. The springs of his benevolence were inexhaustible and could not choose but flow.

Sir James Stephen
Essays in Ecclesiastical Biography
1883

Introduction

I am thankful for the reception accorded my two-volume work, *George Whitefield: The Life and Times of the Great Evangelist of the Eighteenth-Century Revival.* Although each volume of this work amounts to six hundred pages, it has had several printings and has been widely read. Readers in various countries have expressed their gratitude for the information and fascination these books provided. For instance, Dr. Cornelius Van Til of Princeton and Westminster Seminaries in reviewing Volume One stated,

> Read this book. You may forget to talk to your wife (or husband); you may forget to go to work; but it's worth a few sacrifices.
> Why do I go to such extremes? To talk like that is surely abnormal. Yes, it is. But I did get into an unusually abnormal state of mind when I read the book. Besides, I am even now, weeks later, still abnormal.

Notwithstanding the large circulation these books have received, many potential readers, lacking a realization of the interest they would find in them, have told themselves, "Two such large volumes would be too much for me."

Accordingly I have condensed the two volumes into one of less than three hundred pages. This book, though brief and simple, reports many of the memorable and exciting matters of Whitefield's life, and I have endeavored to write in a style that I hope will prove abundantly interesting, even to many who are not in the habit of reading.

I trust, however, that readers of this one-volume work, gaining instruction and blessing from its pages, will be influenced to read the two-volume record of the life and times of George Whitefield, the greatest evangelist since the Apostle Paul.

Arnold A. Dallimore
Cottam, Ontario,
Canada, NOR 1B0

Many Whitefield biographers present his life as an enigma which cannot be explained. This is largely due to a failure to recognize the character of his boyhood environment. . . . Whitefield came from a clerical, educated and cultured ancestry.

Edwin Noah Hardy
George Whitefield, the Matchless Soul-winner

1

Born and Born Again

George Whitefield was born in 1714 in The Bell Inn at Gloucester. A three-story structure with a breadth of some two hundred feet, a busy dining room and tavern, it was the finest hostelry in all that part of England. Its Great Room was used for entertainments and the staging of plays, and several outstanding people were among its patrons.

Under the hand of Thomas Whitefield, George's father, The Bell prospered. The Poor Rate charged against him — an indicator of a man's income — was as high as that of anyone in the parish and twice as high as most.

Thomas and his wife Elizabeth had each been brought up in comfortable circumstances. For some years Thomas's father had lived retired on a country estate, and there Thomas had spent his boyhood. Elizabeth came from two respectable Bristol families, several of her relatives filling important civic offices, and the wills written by some reveal that they were very well off.

The Whitefields saw not only their business prosper, but their family too. There were born to them first five boys, then a girl, and finally the boy they named "George." The home was of an upper-middle class character, and the family was among Gloucester's more prominent citizens.

When George was a child of two, however, his father passed away. His mother took over the management of the Inn, and the business continued to prosper. The Poor Rate that she paid remained at its high level.

Whitefield's first biographer, Dr. Gillies of Glasgow, says: "He was regarded by his mother with a peculiar tenderness, and educated with more than ordinary care." After being put to school at an early age, he attended a school known as "The College," associated with Gloucester Cathedral. At the age of twelve he was enrolled at the school attached to the Whitefields' parish church, St Mary de Crypt. There he first revealed a native eloquence and was chosen to make speeches before the City Council when it visited the school.

What kind of boy was George Whitefield? We have some knowledge of his boyhood from an *Account* that he wrote later, in which he describes his early years. Like John Bunyan and several other outstanding Christians, he undoubtedly exaggerates his tendencies towards evil. Its opening paragraphs read:

I can truly say I was brutish from my mother's womb. Lying, filthy talking, and foolish jesting I was much addicted to. Sometimes I used to curse, if not swear. Stealing from my mother I thought no theft at all. Numbers of Sabbaths have I broken, and generally used to behave myself very irreverently in God's sanctuary. Much money have I spent in plays. Cards and reading romances were my heart's delight. Often have I joined with others in playing roguish tricks.[1]

Yet although he thus speaks, he also testifies:

But such was the free grace of God to me, that though corruption worked so strongly in my soul, yet I can recollect very early movings of the blessed Spirit upon my heart. . . . I had some early convictions of sin, and once, when some persons made it their business to tease me, I immediately retired to my room, and kneeling down with many tears, prayed. . . . Part of the money I used to steal from my parent I gave to the poor, and some books I privately took from others, were books of devotion.[2]

As to his actual behavior one must conclude that Whitefield was no better and no worse than his playmates.

He tells us that he used to run into the Independent Meeting House while the service was in progress and shout, "Old Cole! Old Cole!" — the name of the pastor. But when asked by one of the congregation what business he would undertake, he replied "A minister, but I'll take care not to tell stories in the pulpit like old Cole!" He also says, "I was always very fond of being a clergyman, and used to imitate the ministers reading prayers." Thus the intention to become a minister early played a part in his life.

Several of his father's forebears had attended Oxford University and had spent their lives as priests of the Church of England.[3] George's mother evidently had this prospect in mind for him, and he says, "My mother was very careful of my education, and always kept me in my tender years from intermeddling in the least with the public business." It is evident that although her other children might assist in the Inn, this she considered not good enough for George. He was to attend the University, and it was her hope that he would enter the ministry.

But young Whitefield had dreams of a different nature. His schoolmaster frequently wrote plays, and because of George's dramatic tendency these often gave scope for his special ability. Indeed, George possessed a passion for the activity of the stage, and he says, "I was very fond of reading plays, and have kept myself from school for days together to prepare myself for acting them." He evidently became so engrossed on occasion with practicing not only his own part, but the other parts as well, that he would not even go to school. He would remain home all day, and the next two or three days too, dead to things around him, but wondrously alive to the world he had created in his own imagination.

After Mrs. Whitefield had been a widow for eight years, she remarried. Her new husband, Capel Longden, came from a good family and operated a hardware business not far from The Bell. George said, however, "It proved to be what the world would call an unhappy match as for temporals." Longden appears to have been an unpleasant personality; he was able to push himself into the management of the Inn, and with his coming the business started to suffer. The decline continued till with the passing of three or four years it showed a marked deterioration, and the living standards of the Whitefield family were sorely lowered.

Accordingly by the time George was fifteen, he felt his mother's circumstances would no longer allow her to send him to Oxford, and he told her he wanted to leave school and assist in the Inn. At first she refused, but later, with much reluctance, she submitted. He left school, attending for only one subject. "I put on my blue apron," he stated, "and became professed and common drawer for a year and a half."[4]

Yet he found this life very distasteful. "Seeing the boys go by to school," he declared, "has often cut me to the heart." He still, however, held to the hope of attending Oxford, and anticipating the day he would be a minister he composed sermons in the evenings.

This hope took on a new prospect of being fulfilled when a young man told Mrs. Longden he had attended the University at little cost by entering as a servitor. Overjoyed at the possibility thus opened up she cried, "This will do for my son! George, will you go to Oxford?" And he, equally delighted, immediately responded, "With all my heart I will!" And so it was settled. Like his ancestors, George would enter the University!

He now returned to school and labored diligently at his studies. He also entered into a religious manner of life, guarded his thoughts, words and actions, and during Lent fasted for thirty-six hours. He read much in classical works, studied the Greek New Testament, and attended public worship twice a day.

After being in school again for two years, in the Fall of 1732 Whitefield entered Pembroke College, Oxford. As a servitor, in exchange for tuition and board he did menial tasks for the sons of well-to-do gentlemen. It was a humiliating situation, but he performed his duties with fervor and stated that being used to a public house made him all the more capable at this work.

Before he left Gloucester his brothers had assured him that he would forget his religious practices once he reached Oxford. He indeed soon met pressures to do so, and he tells us,

I had not been long at the University, before I found the benefit of the foundation I had laid in the country for a holy life. I was quickly solicited to join in their excess of riot with several who lay in the same room. God . . . gave me grace to withstand them; and once in particular, it being cold, my limbs were so benumbed by sitting alone in my study, because I would not go out amongst them, that I could scarcely sleep all night. But I soon found the benefit of not yielding: for when they perceived they could not prevail, they let me alone as a singular odd fellow.[5]

It was but a short time, however, before Whitefield had kindred company. There was then a group of religiously earnest students in the University, and such terms as "Bible Moths," "Bible Bigots," "Sacramentarians," "Methodists," and "the "Holy Club" were applied to them. These individuals practiced early rising and lengthy devotions, and they strove for a self-discipline which allowed no moment to be wasted throughout the day. They partook of the Sacrament every Sunday, fasted each Wednesday and Friday, and regularly visited Oxford's two prisons to relieve the needs of the inmates. They were all members of the Church of England and believed that these good works ministered towards the salvation of their souls.

Because he was merely a servitor, Whitefield was not allowed to introduce himself to these men. But when he had been in Oxford almost a year, one of them, Charles Wesley, learning that Whitefield too was religiously earnest, invited him to breakfast. This proved the beginning of an historic friendship and later in life Charles said of it:

> Can I the memorable day forget,
>   When first we by Divine appointment met?
> Where undisturbed the thoughtful student roves
>   In search of truth, through academic groves:
> A modest pensive youth, who mused alone,
>   Industrious the frequented path to shun,
> An Israelite without disguise or art,
>   I saw, I loved, and clasped him to my heart,
> A stranger as my bosom friend caress'd,
>   And unawares received an angel-guest.[6]

This description by Charles Wesley deserves our attention. Whitefield was now nineteen and had fair hair and a very fair countenance, and these features were the striking characteristic of his appearance. Moreover, Charles's words "a modest pensive youth" and "without disguise or art" depict one who was guileless and unaffected. Charles also speaks of him as "an angel-guest." Although Whitefield had been born with a slight squint in one eye, this in no way prevented people from thinking of him as possessing an angelic quality. Indeed, as we shall see, people soon began to refer to him as "the Seraph."

Charles introduced Whitefield to his brother John and to the other members of the Holy Club. Although Whitefield was at first reticent about entering among these men, he soon overcame his fears and before long joined in their activities with fervor. He said of them,

Never did persons strive more earnestly to enter in at the strait gate. They kept their bodies under, even to an extreme. They were dead to the world, and willing to be accounted as the dung and offscouring of all things, so that they might win Christ. Their hearts glowed with the love of God and they never prospered so much in the inner man as when they had all manner of evil spoken against them. . . . I now began, like them, to live by rule, and to pick up the very fragments of my time, that not a moment of it might be lost. Whether I ate or drank, or whatsoever I did, I endeavoured to do all to the glory of God. . . . I left no means unused which I thought would lead me nearer to Jesus Christ.[7]

The Holy Club was at that time little known outside of the University. It was composed of some eight or nine men who met together to assist one another in their academic work and in the strict regime they had set for themselves. John Wesley was their moderator, and his strong presence gave force to their purposes and stimulated the other members in their self-discipline.

During his entire course at Oxford, with the exception of the first eleven months, Whitefield was under the strong influence of the Holy Club.

In his academic work he proved an able student, and his concept of the necessity of diligence is manifest in his statement about the practices of others: "It has often grieved my soul to see so many young students spending their substance in extravagant living, and thereby entirely unfitting themselves for the prosecution of their studies." While many a student wasted his days in frivolity, Whitefield practiced the Holy Club's severe discipline, planning each hour and forcing himself to do as he planned, "that not a moment be lost." His personality became cast in this mold of self-mastery, and in our study of his life a recognition of these habits will help us to understand the otherwise inexplicable immensity of his accomplishments.

While under this influence Whitefield read a book which suddenly altered his entire outlook. It was written by a Scotsman, Henry Scougal, and was entitled *The Life of God in the Soul of Man*. Whitefield knew nothing as yet of the miracle of "the new birth"; he assumed that by performing good works he would place himself on the pathway to Heaven. This book convinced him, however, that all such assumptions were utterly false. The discovery filled him with concern, and he wrote that by it,

God showed me that I must be born again, or be damned! I learned that a man may go to church, say prayers, receive the sacrament, and yet not be a Christian. . . .

Shall I burn this book? Shall I throw it down? Or shall I search it? I did search it, and holding the book in my hand I thus addressed the God of heaven and earth: 'Lord, if I am not a Christian, or if not a real one, for Jesus Christ's sake show me what Christianity is, that I may not be damned at last!'

God soon showed me, for in reading a few lines further, that 'true Christianity is a union of the soul with God, and Christ formed within us,' a ray of divine light was instantaneously darted into my soul, and from that moment, and not till then, did I know I must become a new creature.[8]

Aroused by the solemn realization that he "must be born again," Whitefield began a search for "the life of God" which Scougal stated must be placed within his soul.

Amidst his fears of being eternally lost, he became subject to strange and terrible emotions. He stated,

My comforts were soon withdrawn, and a horrible fearfulness and dread permitted to overwhelm my soul. One morning in particular . . . I felt an unusual impression and weight upon my chest, attended with inward darkness. . . .

God only knows how many nights I have lain upon my bed groaning under the weight I felt, and bidding Satan depart from me. . . . Whole days and weeks have I spent in lying prostrate on the ground. . . .[9]

When the bearing of these difficulties brought no experience of "the life of God," Whitefield undertook still greater self-denial. He left off eating such things as fruits and sweets, and wore a patched gown and dirty shoes. He adopted the customs of a German cult, the Quietists, talking very little and wondering if he should talk at all. Under this burdening of his mind his academic work began to suffer, and his tutor thought he might be going mad.

But Whitefield went further in his efforts. For instance, he says concerning one attempt, "After supper I went into Christ Church Walk, and continued in silent prayer under one of the trees for near two hours, sometimes lying flat on my face. . . . The night being stormy I had great reluctance against staying out so long in the cold."

Still finding only failure in all these efforts, he decided the only other thing he could give up was his association with the Holy Club. "This was a sore trial," he declared, "but rather than not be, as I fancied, Christ's disciple, I resolved to renounce them, though dear to me as my own soul."

Whitefield had been undergoing these strivings since the Autumn of 1734, and with the approach of Lent in the Spring of 1735 matters became still worse. He determined that throughout the six weeks of the holy season he would allow himself little except coarse bread and sage tea without sugar. Though burdened in mind, dangerously weakened in body, unable to do his studies, praying "with strong cryings and tears" and constantly reading his Greek New Testament he pressed into his Lenten devotions with increased zeal.

By the Passion Week, however, he found himself too feeble even to creep upstairs. His physician confined him to bed, and he lay there for seven weeks. Despite his weakened condition he wrote a list of his sins, both past and present, and confessed them before God morning and evening every day. But with all his efforts he obtained no "life of God" within his soul.

But now, when there was nothing else that Whitefield could do, God revealed Himself in grace and granted Whitefield that which he had learned could never be earned. In utter desperation and in rejection of all self-trust, he cast himself on the mercy of God through Jesus Christ, and a ray of faith, granted him from above, assured him he would not be cast out. There, as George Whitefield lay on his sickbed in the dormitory of Pembroke College, or perhaps as he knelt in one of Oxford's open fields, God placed divine life within his soul — life that was holy and everlasting — "the life of God in the soul of man." Whitefield testified concerning this experience:

God was pleased to remove the heavy load, to enable me to lay hold of his dear Son by a living faith, and by giving me the Spirit of adoption, to seal me, even to the day of everlasting redemption.

O! with what joy — joy unspeakable — even joy that was full of and big with glory, was my soul filled when the weight of sin went off, and an abiding sense of the love of God broke in upon my disconsolate soul! Surely it was a day to be had in everlasting remembrance. My joys were like a springtide and overflowed the banks.[10]

Not long before his death, looking back upon this life-transforming event Whitefield declared, "I know the place: it may be superstitious, perhaps, but whenever I go to Oxford I cannot help running to that place where Jesus Christ first revealed himself to me, and gave me the new birth."

During the months of Whitefield's first coming before the world, the church walls reeked wherever he had been announced. Of such popularity there had not been an example, either in the Church or out of it.

Isaac Taylor
Wesley and Methodism
1860

2

Preaching That Startled the Nation

*W*hitefield's conversion had taken place a few weeks after Easter, 1735. He was twenty years old.

His joy was such that he could not contain it. "I fell a writing," he says, "to all my brethren and to my sister, and talked to the students as they came into my room." The gloom was entirely gone from his life. He saw before him the boundless possibilities of growth in Christ, and with glad enthusiasm he leaped to enter into them.

But the months of strain had so undermined his health that it was necessary for him to return to Gloucester to recuperate. He arrived there unwell and penniless, but Gabriel Harris, the mayor of the city, with his wife and son, welcomed him into their home and showed him constant kindness during the months he was with them.

Despite the weakness in his health, he was full of vigor in his spirit. Everything about him seemed new. He found, for instance, a new delight in reading the Bible.

My mind being now more open and enlarged, I began to read the Holy Scriptures upon my knees. . . . This proved meat indeed and drink indeed to my soul. I daily received fresh life, light and power from above.[1]

Prayer now became a rich joy. He states:

Oh, what sweet communion had I daily vouchsafed to me with God in prayer. How often have I been carried out beyond myself when sweetly meditating in the fields! How assuredly have I felt that Christ dwelt in me and I in him. And how did I daily walk in the comforts of the Holy Ghost and was edified and refreshed in the multitude of peace.[2]

Whitefield also sought to "grow in grace and in knowledge" through his reading. He made use of several works of the Reformers and the Puritans, and these books served towards giving him a solid doctrinal understanding. He especially wanted to own *Matthew Henry's Commentary*, but since he was too poor to purchase it, Gabriel Harris, a book dealer, let him take it and pay for it later. This set became his beloved companion, and he used it constantly.

We can visualize him at 5 in the morning in his room over Harris's bookstore. He is on his knees with his Bible, his Greek Testament, and a volume of Matthew Henry spread out before him. With intense concentration he reads a portion in English, studies its words and tenses in the Greek, and then considers Matthew Henry's exposition of the whole. Finally comes his unique practice of "praying over every line and every word" in both the English and the Greek, feasting his mind and his heart upon it till its essential meaning has become a part of his very person. When we shortly see him preaching forty and more hours per week with virtually no time whatsoever for preparation, we may look back upon these days and recognize that he was then laying up a store of knowledge on which he was able to draw amidst the tumult and haste of that later ministry.

Moreover, moved by an increasing zeal, Whitefield witnessed to men and women around him. He says, "God made me instrumental to awaken several young people who soon formed themselves into a little Society and had quickly the honour of being despised at Gloucester as we had been at Oxford." This was an historically important event, for this group at Gloucester was the first Methodist Society in the permanent sense of the word, and it remained a unit of Whitefield's work throughout his life. Numerous further Societies, raised by Whitefield, John and Charles Wesley, and several other workers, were to follow, but this was the first.

Charles Wesley described Whitefield's zeal, saying,

> *He now begins from every weight set free*
> *To make full trial of his ministry;*
> *Breaks forth on every side and runs and flies,*
> *Like kindling flames that from the stubble rise;*
> *Where'er the ministerial Spirit leads,*
> *From house to house the heavenly fire he spreads;*
> *Ranges through all the city-lanes and streets,*
> *And seizes every prodigal he meets.*[3]

Of course such zeal aroused bitter opposition on the part of some persons, but it caused excessive admiration in numerous others. People began to assert that so fervent a youth must enter the ministry, and they urged that he apply for ordination right away.

Although since boyhood Whitefield had entertained the idea that he would one day become a minister, now that he truly knew God, he was filled with a sense of dread concerning the spiritual responsibility that office entailed. He stated,

> God alone knows how deep a concern entering the ministry and preaching was to me. I have prayed a thousand times, till the sweat has dropped from my face like rain, that God ... would not let me enter the Church till he called me and thrust me into his work. I remember once in Gloucester, I know the room, I look up at the window when I am there; I know the bedside and the floor upon which I have lain prostrate. I have said, Lord, I cannot go; I shall be puffed up with pride and fall into the snare of the devil.[4]

He prayed that if he was to enter the ministry, God would further indicate it by supplying the financial means for him to return to Oxford. And from one source after another money came, insomuch that when he had been in Gloucester nine months he went back to the University. His health much improved, he soon completed his course and graduated with the Bachelor's degree.

There now came upon him increasingly the conviction that God was indeed calling him to the ministry. If he had once thought of this undertaking as a mere profession, that concept was now entirely gone. He knew the ministry was a holy labor that a man might truly enter only at the clear call of God. Nevertheless, he was ready to yield all, to give himself completely to God, and he stated:

> It is true I have a difficult task, but God is all-sufficient, to whose almighty protection I humbly commit myself. I give to Him my soul and body to be disposed and worn out in His labours as He shall think meet. I do hence resolve, by His assistance ... to lead a stricter life than ever, to give myself to prayer and the study of the Scriptures. . . . God give me my health, if it be His blessed will. . . . I give myself wholly to Him![5]

Willing now to seek ordination, he returned to Gloucester and applied to the bishop, Dr. Benson. Dr. Benson was one of England's better prelates, and recognizing both Whitefield's ability and his extraordinary earnestness despite his being but twenty-one, he agreed to ordain him.

Although Whitefield still greatly feared the spiritual responsibility of the ministry, he was ordained. The event took place on June 20, 1736 in the magnificent Gloucester Cathedral. He stated: "I attempted to behave myself with unaffected devotion, suitable to the greatness of the office I was to undertake."

He had addressed various small groups, but in keeping with Church of England custom Whitefield had not yet preached. Now that he was in "Holy Orders" he was free to do so, and in a letter to a friend he reported:

> Last Sunday . . . I preached my first sermon, in the church of St Mary de Crypt, where I was baptized. . . . Curiosity drew a large congregation. The sight at first a little awed me, but I was comforted with a heartfelt sense of the divine presence and soon found the unspeakable advantage of having been accustomed to speaking when a boy at school, and of exhorting and teaching the prisoners and poor people whilst at the University. By these means I was kept from being daunted over-much.
>
> As I proceeded I perceived the fire kindled, till at last, though so young and amidst a crowd of those who knew me in my infant childish days, I trust I was enabled to speak with some degree of Gospel authority. Some few mocked, but most for the present seemed struck, and I have since heard that a complaint has been made to the Bishop that I drove fifteen mad the first sermon. The worthy Prelate . . . wished that the madness might not be forgotten before next Sunday.[6]

Such was the effect of Whitefield's first sermon on his hearers, but what, we must ask, was the effect on the young preacher himself? We may be sure it made him conscious he possessed marvelous powers of public address, and he would hardly have been human had he not realized that such abilities could lift him to great prominence and could provide him with the multiple profits arising from success.

But he had not the slightest desire to gain human fame or material wealth. His aims are manifest in several statements he made during those days. For example, his comment, "All I can say is I look for perpetual conflicts and struggles in this life, and I hope for no other peace, only a cross, while on this side of eternity"[7] demonstrates his attitude.

A host of people, however, were continually expressing their admiration. "The people grow," he stated, "too, too fond of me. It is time to be going." Accordingly, on the third day after the triumph of his first sermon he turned from the adulation of Gloucester and set out for the University, determined "to be first a saint and then a scholar at Oxford."

He immediately became the leader of the Holy Club, giving guidance to their program of assisting one another in their studies and to their charitable activities. A wealthy baronet, Sir John Philips, recognizing the work Whitefield was doing, offered to provide him with £30 a year as long as he remained at the University. Whitefield proceeded with studies towards his Master's degree, and declared, "I began to be more than content in my present life and had thoughts of staying at the University for some years."

Whitefield was at Oxford merely a few weeks, however, before he was asked to supply the place of a friend who was the minister at the Chapel of the Tower of London. Although he felt himself unworthy to preach and had never before been in London, he accepted the invitation. Of his first service in the city he wrote, "Almost all seemed to sneer at me on account of my youth. But they soon grew serious and exceedingly attentive, and after I came down showed me great tokens of respect." His ministry at the Tower lasted for two months, and among his hearers there were several young apprentices and certain of the titled persons of London, drawn, he says, by his preaching of "the new birth."

He returned to Oxford, but in no time was invited to supply at the village of Dummer. While he was there, he made a decision which greatly affected the rest of his life: he decided to become a missionary to Georgia.

Georgia had been founded by a philanthropical Englishman, Colonel Oglethorpe. He intended it especially as a place where persons released from debtors' prisons could be resettled and also in which Europeans who had suffered Romanist persecutions might find refuge. Among the party that had sailed for the Colony in 1735 were John and Charles Wesley. The lives of these brothers were remarkable for their firm discipline, and they felt that by enduring the privations to be met in foreign missionary labors they would add to the possibility of saving their own souls.

But Charles, since he possessed a sensitive, poetic nature, could not long bear the trials of the new land, and before seven months had passed he left for home. John, feeling his need of assistance, wrote to Whitefield and urged him to come and help.

Although Whitefield was so happy in his life at Oxford, he carefully considered John's request. He felt he was not yet ready to bear the responsibility of ministering in England and that a period in the Colony would provide him with valuable experience. He also assumed that the ocean voyage, supposedly so harmful to one's health, might actually prove beneficial to his not-too-robust condition. Finally, his stay there would not need to be permanent; since ordination in the Church of England is in two stages — first that of a deacon and then that of a priest — it would be necessary for him to return to England to undergo the second rite.

His decision was in no sense an impulsive one. "When these things were thoroughly weighed," said Whitefield, "I at length resolved to embark for Georgia."

Having made this decision, Whitefield intended to leave for America without delay. But he would find himself detained in England for almost a year, and during that time he would be thrust into a ministry of such a nature that it virtually startled the nation.

He went to Bristol to say farewell, but after preaching on a Sunday people clamored for him to preach every day in the week. Churches immediately became crowded, with many turned away for lack of room. People seeking spiritual advice sought him out constantly at his lodgings, and large offers were made in the hope of enticing him to remain in Bristol.

After four weeks of this ministry, he hastened up to London. But there he learned that he was not to sail until Colonel Oglethorpe himself was also ready to depart.

While waiting for the Colonel, he accepted an invitation to preach at Stonehouse in Gloucestershire. He was there when the Spring in all its glory was coming to the Cotswold countryside, and the heart of Whitefield, alive with a perennial springtime, was moved to spiritual ecstasy.

"Sometimes as I was walking," he wrote, "my soul would make

such sallies as though it would go out of my body. At other times I would be so overpowered with a sense of God's Infinite Majesty that I would be compelled to throw myself on the ground and offer my soul as a blank in his hands, to write on it what he pleased."[8]

Whitefield left at Stonehouse the manuscript of his farewell sermon. This sermon, based on Romans 8:30, reveals that a theological system was already forming in his mind. It was the system long referred to as "Calvinism," but which he preferred to term "the doctrines of grace."

While still waiting for Oglethorpe, Whitefield paid a return visit to Bristol. People heard that he was coming, and "multitudes came on foot and many in coaches a mile without the city to greet him." He was invited to preach in church after church, and he wrote:

> I preached as usual about five times a week . . . it was wonderful to see how the people hung upon the rails of the organ loft, climbed upon the leads of the church, and made the church itself so hot with their breath that steam would fall from the pillars like drops of rain. Sometimes almost as many would go away for want of room as came in, and it was with great difficulty that I got into the desk. . . . Persons of all denominations flocked to hear.[9]

Assuming after four weeks that Oglethorpe must now be ready to sail, he again went up to London. Of course, he was requested to preach, and concerning his waiting period he reported:

> On a Lord's Day I used to preach four times to very large and affected audiences, besides reading prayers twice or thrice, and walking perhaps twelve miles in going backwards and forwards from one church to the other. The sight of the congregations was awful. One might, as it were, walk upon the people's heads. . . . They were all attention and heard like people hearing for eternity.
>
> I now preached generally nine times a week. The early sacraments were exceeding awful . . . how often have we seen Jesus Christ, evidently set forth before us, crucified! On Sunday mornings, long before day, you might see streets filled with people going to church, with their lanthorns in their hands, and hear them conversing about the things of God. Other . . . Churches near at hand would be filled with persons who

could not come where I was preaching, and those who did come were so deeply affected that they were like persons . . . mourning for a first-born child.[10]

Nine of the sermons Whitefield preached during these months were published. They combined solid Biblical substance with plain personal application. They show that he attempted first to reach the mind of the hearer, then to awaken his emotion, and finally to move his will. Here was remarkable preaching, especially from one so young.

From the very beginning of Whitefield's ministry, several of the aristocracy were present at every service. In reference to this early period of his preaching, one of these titled persons wrote:

The preaching of Mr Whitefield excited an unusual degree of attention among persons of all ranks. In many of the city churches he proclaimed the glad tidings of great joy to listening multitudes, who were powerfully affected by the fire which was displayed in the animated addresses of this man of God. Lord and Lady Huntingdon constantly attended wherever he preached and Lady Anne Frankland became one of the first fruits of his ministry among the nobility.[11]

The Duchess of Marlborough, wife of England's great warrior, the Duke of Marlborough (a famous forebear of Sir Winston Churchill), was frequently one of Whitefield's hearers. She largely dominated English social life and was altogether a woman of the world, but in a letter to Lady Huntingdon she stated,

My dear Lady Huntingdon is always so very good to me that I must accept your obliging invitation to accompany you to hear Mr Whitefield. . . . God knows we all need mending and none more than myself. I . . . now hope, in my old days, to obtain mercy from God as I never expect any from the hands of my fellow creatures. The Duchess of Ancaster, Lady Townsend and Lady Cobham were exceedingly pleased with many observations in Mr Whitefield's sermon in St Sepulchre's Church, which has made me lament ever since that I did not hear it, as it might have been the means of doing me some good; for good, alas! I do want, but where, among the corrupt sons and daughters of Adam, am I to find it.[12]

We shall notice later the names and titles of several of the nobility who attended Whitefield's preaching in 1750, some of whom were led to the Savior and became strong witnesses for Christ.

But Whitefield was especially heard by great numbers of the common people. He reported:

> The tide of popularity began to run very high. In a short time I could no longer walk on foot, but was constrained to go in a coach from place to place, to avoid the hosannas of the multitude. They grew quite extravagant in their applauses, and had it not been for my compassionate High Priest, popularity would have destroyed me. I used to plead with him to take me by the hand and lead me unhurt through this fiery furnace. He heard my request and gave me to see the vanity of all commendations but his own.[13]

It is evident that had he so desired, Whitefield could have retained very much of this almost unbounded popularity. He had the goodwill of many of the bishops and similar interest of several of the nobility. Sir John Thorold, a man of large wealth, was steadily friendly and had recently given him a sum of money for his personal use; others of the aristocracy showed him constant favor as well. Moreover, there was the extravagant applause, and it had become the practice of numerous people to term him "the Seraph (the angel)."

In his letters, *Journals*, sermons, and private speech, Whitefield referred to himself as "a Methodist," and a host of men and women counted themselves his followers. The Methodism of Oxford reached but a handful of students and knew no assurance of salvation, and it had died away with the departure of the Wesleys in 1735. But this Methodism arising from Whitefield's ministry was a Methodism of joy and assurance, and this was the Methodism that was to become permanent.

In his concern for the spiritual welfare of the numerous men and women his work had attracted, Whitefield recommended that they be always present at the services and Sacraments of their parish churches. But he also urged them to attend the Religious Societies. These were organizations associated with the Church of England, and as the people flocked to attend, most existing Societies became overcrowded, and several new ones were formed.

Whitefield's labor in London lasted four months. As 1737 drew toward its close, he felt he could no longer postpone his sailing for Georgia. Unable to wait for Colonel Oglethorpe, he announced his departure.

> Oh, what groans and sighs were to be heard when I said, 'Finally, brethren, farewell!' . . . All ranks gave vent to their passions. They would run and stop me in the alleys, hug me in their arms, and follow me with wishful looks. . . . With many others I spent a night in prayer and praise, and in the morning helped to administer the Sacrament. But such a sacrament I never saw. The tears of the communicants mingled with the cup and had not Jesus supported our hearts, our parting would have been almost insupportable.[14]

On December 30, 1737 he boarded his vessel. "God give me," he prayed, "a deep humility, a well-guided zeal, a burning love and a single eye, and then let men or devils do their worst."

I was really happy in my little foreign cure and could have cheerfully remained among them, had I not been obliged to return to England to receive priest's orders and make a beginning towards laying a foundation to the Orphan House. . . . During my stay here the weather was most intensely hot. . . . Seeing others do it I determined to inure myself to hardships, by lying constantly on the ground; which, by use I found so far from a hardship, that, afterward it became so to lie in bed.

George Whitefield
Quoted by Dr. Gillies

3

Missionary to Georgia

W hile *The Whitaker*, carrying Whitefield *to* America, was waiting to sail out of the port of Deal, *The Samuel*, bringing John Wesley *from* America, sailed in.

Wesley had gone to America with one supreme purpose: "My chief motive is the hope of saving my soul." He had assumed that salvation would come by way of the Holy Club type of discipline, and he believed that such practices, assisted by enduring the privations of the New World, would largely accomplish that end.

But he returned to England with these hopes shattered by the realization that salvation was not to be gained by any process of human effort. Now he knew that he must be changed inwardly, and he confessed, "What have I learned? Why, what I least of all suspected, that I who went to America to convert others, was never myself converted to God."

Wesley had learned this truth from the Moravians. These were a German people, a small party of whom had been aboard the vessel that carried him to America. He noticed their willingness to perform menial tasks for other passengers, but his chief surprise came when the vessel encountered a violent storm. A raging sea broke over the ship, and although "A terrible screaming began among the English," these German people — men, women, and children — calmly sang a hymn of trust and praise. But Wesley himself confessed that during the storm, "I was afraid to die!"[1]

During his days in Georgia, Wesley had further associations with the Moravians. They testified concerning a certainty of salvation, and he realized that scholar and clergyman though he was, he was ignorant of the assurance of which they spoke. These were his first contacts with evangelical Christianity, and they had a lasting effect.

John found little but difficulty in Georgia. His days there were brought to a close by an innocent but unwise love affair. He was sued for £1000 for defamation of character and escaped to Charleston, South Carolina, from whence he sailed to England.

Upon landing at Deal John learned that Whitefield's vessel was near at hand. Feeling responsible for having urged Whitefield to go to Georgia, he cast a lot (that is, he wrote the several options on slips of paper and selected one of the papers at random). The lot read, "Let him return to London." He sent him word to this effect, and Whitefield replied stating he could not do so.[2] John then set out for London, and Whitefield set sail for Georgia. The date was February 2, 1738.

Although Wesley says nothing about this, upon reaching London he undoubtedly met with the effects of Whitefield's ministry. He could not but have heard of the tremendous congregations that had flocked to Whitefield's services, of the several nobility who were always in his audiences, of his declaration of the necessity of the new birth, and of the many who had entered that experience under his ministry. And despite his dejection Wesley undoubtedly determined that some measure of such success would yet be his.

While sailing the ocean, Whitefield was chaplain to all who were aboard the *Whitaker*. Besides the crew, there were twenty or so women and children and about one hundred soldiers. This vessel and two other ships that accompanied it were sailing first for Gibraltar, where more soldiers were to be taken aboard. All were then to sail for Georgia, where the soldiers would serve in defending the Colony from the Spaniards in Florida.

On his first morning on board Whitefield declared his intention "to know nothing among them, save Jesus Christ and Him crucified." This brought ridicule from the soldiers and the sailors and their captains.

'The first Lord's Day,' he wrote, 'nothing was to be seen but cards and little heard but cursing and swearing. I could do no more than, whilst I was writing, now and then turn my head by way of reproof to a lieutenant who swore as though he was born of a swearing constitution. Now and then he would take my hint, return my nod with a "Doctor, I ask your pardon" and then return to his swearing and cards again.'[3]

In the face of this unpromising situation, Whitefield began his attempt to reach all on board with the gospel. His tact and zeal are well-expressed in his statement, "Oh, that I may catch them with a holy guile!"

The living conditions on such a vessel were undoubtedly wretched. Whitefield had brought with him many tasty items of food and several medicines, and since there was much sickness among the passengers, he went among them every day dispensing of his supply and giving encouragement. Each morning and evening he read prayers on the open deck, although for the time being he did not attempt to preach, lest he deter the people from attending.

After four days, however, he began a catechism class for the soldiers. Only six or seven were present on the first morning, but the number steadily increased until in a week's time the attendance mounted to twenty, and he added to the study an exposition of the Lord's Prayer. Then, finding this was accepted, he began to preach whenever he read prayers.

To these public efforts Whitefield added personal associations. He "breakfasted with some of the gentlemen" and reported an hour's conversation with another "on our fall in Adam and the necessity of the new birth." He walked at night on the deck in order to talk to the chief mate, and on another occasion "About eleven at night [he] sat down with the sailors in the steerage, and reasoned with them about righteousness, temperance and judgement to come."

Steadily gaining the goodwill of all on board, Whitefield began a daily catechism class for the women and soon added a Bible study. He also had James Habersham, a man he had brought with him, give instruction in elementary education for the children, and he invited any soldiers or sailors who wished to learn to read to attend.

While having "a dish of coffee" with the captain of the soldiers, Whitefield suggested that he would like to bring a short message to the captain and the other gentlemen in the great cabin. The captain shortly agreed and "expressed his appreciation of the good [he] was doing" among his men. Then the captain of the sailors ordered that chairs be set out on the deck and planks laid across them, thus making the deck of the *Whitaker* into a sort of floating chapel. Whitefield had also arranged "to meet any soldiers who could sing by note, to join in Divine Psalmody every day," thereby undoubtedly supplying his meeting with a male choir. And daily he preached to almost all on board.

The ship docked first at Gibraltar, and the change on board was widely noticeable. Although but seven weeks earlier the men had been a scornful, cursing company, they now "stood forth like little children to say their Catechism," many read their Bibles regularly, and almost all attended services both morning and evening. Such were the fruits of Whitefield's labor in that short period of time. And when he left Gibraltar "many came to him, weeping, telling him what God had done for their souls," and bringing him gifts.

As the journey to Georgia continued, two vessels sailing with the *Whitaker* frequently drew close, and Whitefield preached to the companies on all three ships. What a sight this must have been — the three decks ablaze with the red coats of the soldiers, and the young chaplain standing with the naval and military captains at his side as he declared the Word of God to all.

Before Georgia was reached, an epidemic of fever swept over the ship. For many days and nights Whitefield visited the several sick ones; but, as was to be expected, he contracted the disease himself. He lay at the doors of death for some days, but from this extremity God brought him back. "He saw I was not yet ripe for glory," he wrote, "and therefore in mercy spared me."

Finally, four months after leaving England, the vessel dropped anchor on the coast of Georgia.

At this date — May 17, 1738 — the Colony was but six years old. The one chief settlement was Savannah, but Colonel Oglethorpe soon arrived and commenced another — Frederica, about one hundred miles further south. The total population of the Colony was approximately one thousand, and it was to minister among this small company that Whitefield had left his crowds in London.

Although still sick from the fever suffered aboard ship, Whitefield held his first service at 5 the next morning. There were seventeen adults and twenty-five children present. Wesley's chief opponent, Thomas Causton, the chief magistrate, "promised to build him a house and showed him much favour."

In his first letter to Harris of Gloucester he said, "America is not so horrid a place. The heat of the weather, lying on the ground, etc. are mere painted lions in the way, and to a soul filled with divine love are not worth mentioning."

Colonel William Stephens, the secretary of the Colony, made the following entries in his official *Journal*:

June 4. Mr Whitefield's auditors increase daily, and the place of worship is too small to contain the people who seek his doctrine.

June 18. Mr Whitefield went on moving the people with his captivating discourses. A child being brought to church to be baptized, he performed that office by sprinkling, which gave great content to many who had taken great distaste at the form of dipping so obstinately withstood by some parents that they have suffered their children to go without the benefit of the sacrament, till a convenient opportunity could be found of another minister to do that office.

July 2. Mr Whitefield gains more and more on the affections of the people, by his labour and assiduity in the performance of divine offices; to which an open and easy deportment, without show of austerity, or singularity of behaviour in conversation, contribute not a little.[4]

This visit to Georgia, however, had an important effect on Whitefield's life. Several of the settlers had died and had left numerous orphans; they were in a homeless condition, and he determined to return to England and secure a charter and money to establish an Orphan House for them.

In view of this intention, after five months Whitefield brought his ministry in the Colony to a close. Colonel Stephens, in reporting his final service, said, "The congregation was so crowded that a great many stood without the doors and under the windows . . . pleased with nothing more than the assurance he gave of his intention to return as soon as possible."

Whitefield's voyage to England was a long and frightening affair. A great storm soon struck, and the mainsail and tackling were ruined, and the fresh provisions were washed overboard. Another vessel, speedier and well-provisioned, came by and, learning of Whitefield's presence, invited him aboard. But feeling it unfitting for a Christian to escape from danger while others were left to endure it, he declined.

The ship proved a place of hunger and thirst, and above all it became lost on the immensity of the ocean. During the third month there suddenly rang out the cry of, "Land! Land!" They had reached the coast of Ireland, and when a boat went ashore, a great gentleman sent word for Whitefield to spend some days with him recuperating.

But Whitefield had no time to spend resting his physical person and set out across Ireland. Arriving at Limerick, he was made a guest of the mayor, and the bishop had him preach at the Cathedral. At Dublin the bishop invited him to dine, and the archbishop received him with much courtesy.

Finally, on November 30, 1738, he reached the port of Parkgate in England. Eleven months had elapsed since his tearful farewell in London.

As the scene was quite new, it often occasioned many inward conflicts. The open firmament above me, the prospect of the adjacent fields, with the sight of thousands and thousands, some in coaches, some on horseback and some in the trees, and at times all affected and drenched in tears together, to which sometimes was added the solemnity of the approaching evening, was almost too much for, and quite overcame me.

George Whitefield
1739

It was a brave day for England when Whitefield began field preaching.

C. H. Spurgeon

4

Into the Open Air

T
he news that Whitefield was again in England was greeted
with joy by his friends. Charles Wesley was in Oxford at the
time, and he quickly made his way to London. John Wesley,
who was in the same area, wrote, "Hearing Mr Whitefield was
arrived from Georgia I hastened to London. . . . God gave us once
more to take sweet counsel together."

During Whitefield's absence the Wesleys had each been converted.
They had been in contact with a Moravian minister, Peter Bohler, and
he had impressed on them that nothing they could do would save
their souls and that salvation came only through faith in Christ. In
fear of being eternally lost, the brothers then made the search for faith
the burning desire of their lives. But though they yearned to receive
faith, they knew not how to do so.

Charles was aided by a book, Martin Luther's *Commentary on
Galatians*, which a layman, William Holland, brought and read with
him. As they came upon Luther's statement, "What, have we nothing
to do? No! Nothing! but only accept of him 'who of God is made
unto us wisdom and righteousness and sanctification and redemption,'" Holland was so overcome with joy that he declared, "I could
scarce feel the ground I trod upon."[1]

As days and nights went by, Charles prayed and longed for faith,
and he felt Christ might appear in human form to bring it to him. He
soon came to the end of all hope of saving his own soul, and on the
morning of Sunday, May 21, 1738 he trusted solely in Christ and
entered into the assurance of salvation. Filled with delight, he wrote
a hymn to commemorate the occasion, and it may well have been his
grand composition that begins,

And can it be that I should gain,
An interest in the Saviour's blood?

Three days later John came into the same experience. As is widely known, he was present at a Society in Aldersgate Street where "one was reading Luther's preface to his commentary on the epistle to the Romans." The reader was undoubtedly William Holland, and Wesley states that as he read,

> I felt my heart strangely warmed. I felt I did trust in Christ, Christ alone for salvation; and an assurance was given me that he had taken away my sins, even mine, and saved me from the law of sin and death.[2]

The experience of the new birth proved a great turning point in the life of each of the brothers. For Charles, conversion especially opened the fountain of poetic composition that was part of his very nature, and a virtual stream of hymns began to flow from his pen — hymns that have strengthened, beautified, and elevated Christian singing from that day till this.

John likewise experienced victory and spiritual joy. But seeking further enlightenment he paid a visit to the Moravian headquarters at Herrnhut in Germany, and upon his return to London he was something of a Moravian himself. In a letter to Herrnhut he stated,

> We are endeavouring here also . . . to be followers of you as you are of Christ. . . . Though my brother and I are not permitted to preach in most of the churches in London, yet, 'thanks be to God' there are others left wherein we have liberty to speak the truth as it is in Jesus. Likewise on every evening . . . we publish the word of reconciliation, sometimes to twenty or thirty, sometimes to fifty or sixty, sometimes to three or four hundred persons, met together to hear it.[3]

The fact that Whitefield was again in London drew not only the Wesleys to greet him. Four other Holy Club men came also. The seven entered with intense fervor into the already ardent meetings of the Fetter Lane Society, and we feel something of their enthusiasm as we read Whitefield's report:

> Sometimes whole nights were spent in prayer. Often have we been filled as with new wine. And often have we seen them overwhelmed

with the Divine presence and crying out, "Will God indeed dwell with men upon earth! How dreadful is this place! This is none other than the house of God and the gate of Heaven!"[4]

But John Wesley had a still more striking account of their fellowship. On New Year's night, as they met with "about sixty brethren" for the Moravian Love Feast,

> About three in the morning, as we were continuing instant in prayer, the power of God came mightily upon us, insomuch that many cried out for exceeding joy, and many fell to the ground. As soon as we were recovered a little from that awe and amazement at the presence of His majesty, we broke out with one voice, 'We praise Thee, O God; we acknowledge Thee to be the Lord!'[5]

Early in January Whitefield went to Oxford to enter the second stage of the Church of England's ordination: that of a priest. The rite was performed by Bishop Benson, the prelate who had ordained him a deacon. Dr. Benson had already spoken of Whitefield as "a well-meaning young man, with good abilities and great zeal," and had prayed that "God would grant him great success in all his undertakings for the . . . revival of true religion in these degenerative days." Whitefield received this second ordination with the same awesome sense of spiritual responsibility as he had the first.

The opposition that had been somewhat evident against Whitefield before he went to Georgia had increased noticeably during his absence. Formerly several of the clergy had merely tolerated him, assuming that as soon as he left England his influence would die away.

But they found the very opposite to be true. During his absence, his hosts of followers in Bristol, in Gloucester, and in London continued to hold him in high admiration and to pray that he would soon return. Nine of the sermons he had preached were published, and one on "The New Birth" received a very large circulation and became something of a manifesto of the Methodist movement. Moreover, a *Journal* of his voyage to America had also been published — this without his knowledge — three publishers giving it their own edition. By these means, although without the least design on his part, he was kept before the public.

Whitefield had previously used several churches, preaching and receiving offerings for Georgia. As he returned, he assumed the churches would be even more available, for he was now speaking on behalf of orphans. But on his second day in London he stated, "Five churches have already been denied me, and some of the clergy would oblige me to depart out of these coasts."

Nevertheless, he had a tremendous ministry. He preached in a total of fifteen churches, but it was in the Religious Societies that he found his greatest labor. Something of his constant activity is evident in the following report:

Preached nine times this week, and expounded near eighteen times. . . . I am every moment employed from morning till midnight. There is no end of people coming to me, and they seem more and more desirous, like new-born babes, to be fed with the sincere milk of the Word.[6]

Whitefield felt, however, that this situation might not long continue. He felt that both he and the Wesleys might soon be denied the use of all the churches, and might even be prevented from ministering in the Societies. Accordingly, after knowing that a host of people had stood outside a church while he had preached within, he said, "This put me first upon thinking of preaching without doors. I mentioned it to some friends who looked upon it as a mad notion. However, we kneeled down and prayed that nothing may be done rashly."[7]

But the idea of preaching out-of-doors did not originate with Whitefield. It came to him through correspondence with a tireless, fearless, dynamic Welshman, Howell Harris.

Harris, a schoolteacher, had been converted about the same time as Whitefield. Although he was a layman and therefore not allowed to preach, he began to gather people together in private homes and declared to them what God had done for his soul.

Harris soon went further. He attended various outdoor events — such things as fairs and sporting matches — and, using anything as a platform — a horse block, a stone wall, or a table placed on the street — he preached the gospel. His efforts were marked by tremendous zeal, and the blessing of God was abundantly upon him. He was bitterly opposed by magistrates and clergy, but mighty conviction and glorious conversion accompanied his work, and much of South Wales became aware of this fervent man and his message.

Because he was unordained, Harris did not call his work preaching; he referred to it only as "exhorting." But he resigned from teaching school and devoted himself totally to this labor, and we catch something of his spirit from his statement,

> A strong necessity was laid upon me that . . . I must go to the utmost to exhort. I could not meet or travel with anybody . . . without speaking to them concerning their souls. I went during the festive season from house to house in our parish. . . .
>
> My food and my drink was praising God. A fire was kindled in my soul and I was clothed with power. . . . I could have spoken to the King were he within my reach. . . . I lifted up my voice with authority, and fear and terror would be seen on all faces. . . . I thundered greatly, denouncing the gentry, the carnal clergy and everybody.[8]

Shortly after his return from Georgia, Whitefield heard of Harris and wrote to him. Harris replied, and it was evident that here were two men of kindred spirit and similar work.

Whitefield determined to go to Wales to meet Harris, accompany him as he conducted some of his open-air meetings, and watch him as he performed his tremendous task.

Whitefield took with him on this trip a young gentleman, William Seward, the son of a country squire. Seward had attained financial success in the stock market and had given extensively in the support of Charity Schools. In seeking spiritual help he had met Charles Wesley, and Charles soon reported, "William Seward testified faith." But when Whitefield returned from America, Seward became so devoted to him that he offered to place his fortune at his disposal and to accompany him wherever he might go.

On the way to Wales, Whitefield called at the home of the Rev. and Mrs. Westley Hall. Mrs. Hall was the sister of John and Charles Wesley, and their widowed mother, Susanna, was living with the Halls at the time. In a letter to her other son, Samuel, Susanna told of Whitefield's visit and stated, "He seems to be a very good man, and one who really desires the salvation of mankind. God grant that the wisdom of the serpent may be joined with the innocency of the dove."[9]

After arriving in Bristol, Whitefield found himself so busied in preaching in the Religious Societies and the jail that he put off, for the time being, going on to Wales.

He decided, however, to attempt open-air ministry. Adjacent to Bristol there lay a large coal mining district, Kingswood. It contained several hundreds of miners — colliers — and they, with their women and children, labored long hours at their grimy work. Neither school nor church had ever been built for them, outsiders seldom entered their district, and there had been occasions on which they had stormed into Bristol in violence.

Although the month was February and that Winter was the coldest in memory, on the first Saturday after reaching Bristol Whitefield and Seward went out to Kingswood. They visited from hovel to hovel, inviting the people to gather, and Whitefield reported, "I went upon a mount and spake to as many as came to me. There were upwards of two hundred."

Upon returning to Bristol, Whitefield reflected on what he had done. He knew such an action on the part of a clergyman would be considered the height of fanaticism, but he stated,

> Blessed be God! I have broken the ice. I believe I was never more acceptable to my Master than when I was standing to teach those hearers in the open fields. Some may censure me, but if I thus pleased men I should not be the servant of Christ.[10]

On the following Wednesday Whitefield went out again to Kingswood, and this time the crowd was estimated at two thousand. He was there again on Friday, and now his hearers were believed to number four thousand. And on Sunday, after preaching at 6 in the morning, reading prayers in a church at 8, preaching at 10, and preaching again in a churchyard, he reported, "At four I hastened to Kingswood. At a moderate computation there were about ten thousand people. . . . The trees and hedges were full. All was hush when I began; the sun shone bright, and God enabled me to preach for an hour with great power, and so loudly that all, I was told, could hear."[11] He concluded the day by preaching at two more Societies. "About nine I came home, rejoicing at the great things God had done for my soul."

During these days in Bristol, Whitefield stayed at the home of his sister, a widow, and their mother frequently visited. Not surprisingly, Mrs. Longden marveled at the great prominence her son had received.

Whitefield also now paid his intended visit to Wales and met

Howell Harris. They each leaned toward an acceptance of Calvinistic theology and were alike also in zeal. Whitefield reported that Harris "had established nearly thirty Societies in South Wales" — a work begun a year before Whitefield began to preach and two years before the Wesleys were converted.

Although outsiders had long been afraid to enter the colliers' district, Whitefield never faced a threatening word or gesture among them. On the contrary, they seem to have held him in true affection, and in a description that has become classic he reported the effects of his work among them, saying,

> Having no righteousness of their own to renounce, they were glad to hear of a Jesus who was a friend of publicans and sinners, and came not to call the righteous but sinners to repentance. The first discovery of their being affected was to see the white gutters made by the tears which plentifully fell down their black cheeks, as they came out of their coal pits. Hundreds and hundreds of them were soon brought under deep convictions, which, as the event proved, happily ended in a sound and thorough conversion.[12]

Whitefield was now holding some thirty meetings a week in and around Bristol. Six weeks, however, was all the time he could give to this work, and therefore he looked for a man who could come and conduct it. He thought of two or three, but considered them unsuitable. So he wrote to John Wesley, urging him to come. But though Wesley was intrigued with the possibilities of open-air preaching, he was too strict in the proprieties of the Church of England to go readily. He and the men of the Fetter Lane Society accepted the first verse their eye lighted upon after opening their Bibles as the direction of God to them in the matter. Four times they came upon a verse that spoke of suffering or death, and Wesley believed that were he to go to Bristol he would die. Nevertheless he declared, "I go," and Charles stated, "I desired to die with him."

After reaching Bristol John reported,

> Brother Whitefield expounded on Sunday morning to six or seven thousand at the Bowling Green; at noon to much the same number at Hanham Mount, and at five to, I believe, thirty thousand from a little mount in Rose Green. . . .

I could scarce reconcile myself at first to this strange way of preaching in the fields . . . having been all my life . . . so tenacious of every point relating to decency and order, that I should have thought the saving of souls a sin if it had not been done in a church.[13]

Whitefield had announced that there would be a service again at a place known as the Brickyard or the Glass Houses. At the given hour people would be there waiting for him, but he planned that instead of going himself he would have Wesley go, thus thrusting him into preaching in the open air. Wesley went, saw the crowd, and reluctantly preached. This was the beginning of activity which consumed much of the rest of his life.

Knowing that Whitefield was about to depart for London, the Kingswood colliers arranged a farewell for him. "They prepared," he says, "a very hospitable entertainment." Since he had suggested building a school for them, "they were now very forward for [him] to lay the first stone." A man had donated a piece of ground, a stone was provided, and, kneeling upon it, Whitefield prayed that "the gates of hell might not prevail against the design." The colliers gave "above twenty pounds in money and forty pounds in subscriptions," and they also promised their labor and such materials as they might possess.

After this farewell in Kingswood, satisfied that the work he had begun in and around Bristol would be ably carried on, Whitefield left for London.

Wesley then took over the leadership of the Bristol work. He did not possess Whitefield's great organ-like voice nor his dramatic oratory, but although his congregations were smaller, his intellectual concentration and strength of will came into play as he preached and gave his ministry unusual force. Now that he had become an open-air preacher, all was changed for him, and he saw before him the possibility of reaching hosts of men and women everywhere with the gospel and of building a widespread movement. He revealed his vision when, as he stood before a Bristol congregation, he declared, "I could have cried out (in another sense than poor vain Archimedes) 'Give me where to stand and I will shake the earth!'"[14]

Nothing could more forcibly have indicated Wesley's purpose: "Give me where to stand and I will shake the earth."

And the Lord said unto the servant, Go out into the highways and hedges, and compel them to come in, that my house may be filled.

Luke 14:23

Let not the adversaries say I have thrust myself out. No; they have thrust me out. And since the self-righteous men of this generation count themselves unworthy, I go out into the highways and hedges, and compel harlots, publicans and sinners to come in, that my Master's house may be filled.

George Whitefield
1741

5

Into the Open Air in London

On his first Sunday morning after reaching London, Whitefield preached in the open air in a park-like place called Moorfields. Notice had been given of his coming and

... he found an incredible number of people assembled. Many had told him he would never come out of that place alive. He went in between two friends who by pressure of the crowd were soon entirely parted from him and were obliged to leave him to the mercy of the rabble. But these, instead of hurting him, formed a lane for him and carried him along to the middle of the Fields (where a table had been placed which was broken to pieces by the crowd) and afterwards back again to the wall that parted the upper and lower Moorfields; from whence he preached without molestation to an exceedingly great multitude.[1]

In this action Whitefield introduced Methodism to Moorfields, a location which has been its chief center ever since.

That evening Whitefield chose his second London location, Kennington Common. The Common was a large open field where great numbers of the poor gathered. It held a permanent scaffold on which hangings were frequently conducted. Vicious sports and drunken brawlings were prevalent. Here men, women and children, unwashed, ignorant, and diseased, were to be found in abundance, and "no man cared for their souls." Whitefield reported that on that evening,

No less than thirty thousand were supposed to be present. The wind being for me carried my voice to the extremest part of the audience. All stood attentive and joined in the Psalm and the Lord's Prayer most regularly. I scarce ever preached more quietly in a church. The Word came with power. . . . I hope a good inroad has been made into the devil's kingdom to-day.[2]

Satisfied with this initial step into the open air in London, Whitefield returned to Kennington each evening and to Moorfields each Sunday morning. We follow his amazing labors as reported in his *Journals*:

Wednesday, May 2. Preached this evening to above 10,000 at Kennington Common. . . .

Saturday, May 5. Preached yesterday and to-day as usual at Kennington Common, to about twenty thousand hearers, who were very much affected.

Sunday, May 6. Preached this morning in Moorfields to about twenty thousand people, who were very quiet and attentive, and much affected. Went to public worship morning and evening, and at six preached at Kennington. Such a sight I never saw before. I believe there were no less than fifty thousand people, and near four score coaches, besides great numbers of horses. God gave me great enlargement of heart. I continued my discourse for an hour and a half, and when I returned home I was filled with such love, peace and joy that I cannot express it.

Tuesday, May 8 . . . before I set out from town it rained very hard. . . . To my great surprise, when I came to the Common I saw above twenty thousand people. All the while . . . the sun shone upon us; and I trust the Sun of Righteousness arose on some with healing in his wings.

Wednesday, May 9 . . . after God had enabled me to preach to about twenty thousand for above an hour at Kennington, He inclined the hearers' hearts to contribute most cheerfully and liberally to the Orphan House. . . . When we came home we found that we had collected above £46, amongst which were £16 in half pence.

Thursday, May 10. Preached at Kennington, but it rained most of the day. There were not above ten thousand people and thirty coaches. However, God was pleased so visibly to interpose in causing the weather to clear up and the sun to shine out just as I began, that I could not avoid taking notice of it in my discourse.

Friday, May 11. Preached at Kennington to a larger audience than last night, and collected £26 15s. 6d. for the Orphan House. The people offered willingly. Being upon the Publican and the Pharisee, I was very earnest in endeavouring to convince the self-righteous Pharisees of this generation, and offering Jesus Christ freely to all, who, with the humble publican feelingly cry out, "God be merciful to me a sinner."

Saturday, May 12 . . . Many came to me this morning, acquainting me what God had done for their souls by my preaching in the fields. In the evening I preached to about twenty thousand at Kennington. . . . I offered Jesus Christ to all who could apply him to their hearts by faith. . . . The Lord make them willing in the day of His power!

Sunday, May 13. Preached this morning to a prodigious number of people in Moorfields and collected for the orphans £52 19s. 6d. above £20 of which was in half pence . . . they were more than one man could carry home. Went to public worship twice (in a Church of England) and preached in the evening to near sixty thousand people. Many went away because they could not hear, but God enabled me to speak so that the best part of them could understand me well, and it is very remarkable what a deep silence is preserved whilst I am speaking. After sermon I made another collection of £29 17s. 8d., and came home deeply humbled.[3]

While conducting this work, Whitefield was besieged with invitations to come and preach at other places too. He responded to as many as possible and exclaimed, "Blessed be God! we begin to surround this great city!" He also spent a week conducting a preaching tour to cities to the north of London, and remarked, "Many sinners have been convicted and many saints comforted. I find there are some thousands of secret ones . . . who have not bowed the knee to Baal, and this public way of acting brings them out."

Upon returning to London, Whitefield continued his ministry with still greater urgency. He had already booked his passage to America, and the vessel expected to sail within two weeks. The people flocked to hear him in greater numbers than ever and he reported:

Sunday, May 27. Preached this morning at Moorfields to about twenty thousand. . . . My discourse was about two hours long. My heart was full of love and people were so melted down on every side that the greatest scoffer must have owned this was the finger of God . . . preached in the evening at Kennington Common to about the same number as last Lord's Day. I was a little hoarse, but God strengthened me to speak, so as not only to be heard, but felt. . . .

Monday, May 28. Preached . . . at Hackney in a field, to about ten thousand people. I insisted much on the reasonableness of the doctrine of the new birth. . . . Great numbers were in tears. . . .

Tuesday, May 29. Preached at Kennington to a devout auditory, with much sweetness and power. . . .

Wednesday, May 30 . . . preached in the evening at Newington Common, to about fifteen thousand people. A very commodious place was erected for me to preach from . . . seeing a great multitude I thought proper to collect for the Orphan House, and £16 9s. 4d. was gathered.

Thursday, May 31. Was taken ill this afternoon, but God was pleased to strengthen me to go to Kennington. . . .

Friday, June 1 . . . preached in the evening at a place called Mayfair, near Hyde Park Corner. The congregation, I believe, consisted of near eighty thousand people. In the time of my prayer there was a little noise, but they kept a deep silence during the whole of my discourse. A high and very commodious scaffold was erected for me to stand upon, and though I was weak in myself, yet God strengthened me to speak so loud that most could hear, and so powerfully that most, I believe, could feel. All love, all glory, be to God through Christ!

Saturday, June 2 . . . Collected by private contributions nearly £50 for the orphans, and preached in the evening to about ten thousand at Hackney, where £20 12s. 4d. was gathered.

Sunday, June 3. Preached at Moorfields to a larger congregation than ever, and collected £29 17s. 9d. for the Orphans. Went twice to public worship. . . . Preached in the evening at Kennington Common to the most numerous audience I ever yet saw in that place, and collected £34 5s. When I mentioned my departure they were melted into tears. . . . Oh what marvellous kindness has God shown me in this great city![4]

The Rev. Luke Tyerman, a man devoutly loyal to John Wesley, and the most prolific of all writers of Methodist history, after presenting the above reports, stated,

. . . it may be useful to pause and to ponder these marvellous extracts from the young preacher's Journal. Are they not unique? is there any man, except Whitefield, whose diary for so many consecutive days, contains a series of statements like the foregoing?[5]

One would assume that following so extensive a course of meetings Whitefield would be physically and mentally exhausted. It would be expected that to stand before these multitudes ten or more times a week, to overcome the opposition of the unruly, to command the attention of all, to meet the inclemencies of wind and rain and preach for an hour, or perhaps two, would have left him overcome with fatigue. An English essayist, John Foster, in considering the vocal effort alone remarked:

> With all the advantage of such a power of voice as perhaps no other man possessed, there must still often have been the necessity of forcing it to the last possibility of exertion, in order to enable his being heard by congregations amounting to many thousands. . . .[6]

Yet, the fact is that Whitefield makes no suggestion of weariness as the result of these labors. The sight of the crowds and the prospect of preaching to them had an exhilarating effect on his mind, and both during and after his great efforts in the fields he frequently experienced a richly increased joy and strength. He made several such reports, saying for example,

> When we came home . . . God was pleased to pour into my soul a great spirit of supplication, and a sense of His free, distinguishing mercies so filled me with love, humility, joy and holy confusion, that I could at last only pour out my heart before Him in an awful silence. I was so full I could not well speak. Oh the happiness of communion with God![7]

Of course, the question as to the actual number of Whitefield's hearers must be considered. We notice the figures he gives, stating he preached on several occasions to twenty-five thousand, and at times his estimate runs as high as forty thousand and once to eighty thousand. Are these figures accurate?

The *Gentleman's Magazine*, reporting one of his meetings, stated that his audience "covered three acres" — 14,520 square yards. Another periodical described one of his congregations as "a prodigious concourse," and other contemporaries used the terms "most numerous" and "an innumerable multitude." Even his opposers left testimony in the matter. Dr. Trapp, a prominent London clergyman, made reference to "vast multitudes . . . so sottish as to run madding after him," and the Rev. Thomas Church asserted, "He cannot possibly be supposed to know all . . . those present at his meetings of 30, 50 or 80,000."

When, in a few months, Whitefield again reached America, Benjamin Franklin measured the distance at which his voice could be heard, and stated, "I computed he might well be heard by more than thirty thousand." But although we consider Franklin's figure too high, and if we reduce Whitefield's by half, still we are left with congregations that, before the electrical amplification of sound, were undoubtedly the largest ever reached by a human voice in all history. And this was the work of a youth of twenty-four!

One of Whitefield's chief accomplishments during these days was his leading Charles Wesley into the open-air ministry. Charles was happily engaged in doing personal work among a number of acquaintances and in preaching at a few churches and Societies. But the labor of preaching to the surging crowds in Moorfields and Kennington was a responsibility of a very different nature, one that he was not ready to accept.

Accordingly, Whitefield sought to press him into the task. He had him stand with him before some of his open-air congregations. "I attended G. Whitefield to Blackheath," he wrote of such an occasion. "He preached in the rain to many listening sinners."

A few days later Charles visited a country district, and while he was there he made his own first attempt. "Franklyn, a farmer, invited me to preach in his field. I did so to about five hundred on 'Repent, for the kingdom of heaven is at hand.' I returned to the house rejoicing."

Yet after returning to London Charles hesitated to take the momentous step there. It meant a deep self-renunciation and a fearful burden of labor, and for a person of so poetic a nature and such adherence to churchly proprieties, the decision abounded with difficulties.

But Whitefield would not brook a long delay. Indeed, he finally informed Charles that he expected him to preach the following Sunday morning to his own congregation which would be waiting for him in Moorfields. Charles confessed,

My inward conflict continued. I perceived it was the fear of man, and that by preaching in the field next Sunday as George Whitefield urges me, I shall break down the bridge and become desperate. I retired and prayed ... for Christ's sake and the Gospel's. I was somewhat less burdened, yet could not be quite easy till I gave up all.[8]

Whitefield understood his man, however, and knew that since Charles was a Wesley, he could not long remain in fear of any situation. As expected, Charles did become "desperate" and broke down the bridge that Sunday, recording,

> I prayed and went forth in the name of Jesus Christ. I found near ten thousand helpless sinners waiting for the Word in Moorfields. I invited them in my Master's name 'Come unto me, all ye that travail and are heavy laden, and I will give you rest.' . . . My load was gone and all my doubts and scruples. God shone upon my path, and I knew this was His will concerning me.[9]

Two weeks later Charles stepped fully into Whitefield's Sunday labors, preaching to "near ten thousand" at Moorfields in the morning and to "double that number" at Kennington in the evening. "The Lord Almighty bowed their hearts before Him," he exclaimed.

Yet the struggle was not over by any means. Charles continued to preach in the open air, but he faced the task of adjusting to the life of extraordinary labor and the new measure of success and popularity that it brought. He stated,

> I never till now knew the strength of temptation and the energy of sin. Who that conferred with flesh and blood would covet great success? I live in a continual storm. My soul is always in my hand. . . . Too well pleased with my success, which brought upon me the buffetings of Satan.[10]

Recognizing Whitefield's leadership in the work, Charles felt he should inform him that he was uneasy about the responsibility Whitefield had thrust upon him.

> "I am continually tempted to leave off preaching," he wrote. ". . . God continues to work *by* me but not *in* me, that I can perceive. Do not reckon upon me, my brother, in the work God is doing. . . . I rejoice in your success, and pray for its increase a thousandfold."[11]

But Charles's retreat was only in words. He continued the ministry in the fields and became a preacher of extraordinary power. The blessing of God was on his labors, and he could say, "Every day we hear of more and more convinced and pardoned."

Having found no one to take over the Gloucester work, Whitefield had Charles make a preaching tour of the area. The new measure of self-renunciation that the field preaching required was now vividly illustrated. During their Oxford days Charles and John had been friendly with two cultured families who lived near Gloucester, the Granvilles and the Kirkhams. But Charles reports that now,

> An old acquaintance (Mrs. Kirkham) stood in my way, and challenged me, 'What, Mr Wesley, is it you I see? Is it possible that you who can preach at Christ Church, St Mary's, &c., should come hither after a mob?' I cut her short with, 'The work which my Master giveth me, must I not do it' and went to my mob, or (to put it in the Pharisees' phrase) this people which is accursed. Thousands heard me gladly, while I told them of their privilege of the Holy Ghost, and exhorted them to come for Him to Christ as poor lost sinners. I continued my discourse till night.[12]

Charles became an open-air preacher of great power. A layman described his ministry, saying,

> I found him standing on a table-board . . . with his hands and eyes lifted up to heaven in prayer; he prayed with uncommon fervency, fluency, and variety of proper expressions. He then preached about an hour in such a manner as I scarce ever heard any man preach. Though I have heard many a finer sermon, according to the common taste . . . I never heard any man discover such evident signs of a vehement desire, or labour so earnestly to convince his hearers that they were all by nature in a sinful, lost, undone state. He showed how great a change a faith in Christ would produce in the whole man.
>
> With uncommon fervour he acquitted himself as an ambassador of Christ, beseeching them in his name . . . to be reconciled to God. Although he used no notes nor had anything in his hand but a Bible, yet he delivered his thoughts in a rich copious variety of expression, and with so much propriety, that I could not observe any thing incoherent . . . through the whole performance.[13]

Years later, as he reflected on the days when he had first undertaken the open-air work, in lines addressed to Whitefield Charles
wrote,

> *Nor did I linger at my friend's desire,*
>   *To tempt the furnace and abide the fire;*
> *When suddenly sent forth, from the highways*
>   *I called poor outcasts to the feast of grace;*
> *Urged to pursue the work by thee begun,*
>   *Through good and ill report, I still rushed on,*
> *Nor felt the fire of popular applause,*
>   *Nor feared the torturing flame in such a glorious cause.*[14]

Wesley's genius for government was not inferior to that of Richelieu.

Lord Macaulay
1832

Powers like Wesley's produce an inward restlessness, and a perpetual uneasy sense of discontent, till they find or force their way into action.

Robert Southey
England's Poet-Laureate
1820

6

Doctrinal Differences and Sad Divisions

I t has long been recognized that there were doctrinal differences between John Wesley and George Whitefield, and the point we have now reached in our narrative is that at which a separation came about between the two men. Since this affair played a highly important part in their lives, we have no choice but to look into it. It has, however, generally been reported in a manner strongly biased in Wesley's favor, and therefore we must attempt to rectify matters to some extent.

Wesley separated first from the Moravians. He was at the time in association with the Fetter Lane Religious Society, but this body, under the instruction of Peter Bohler, was fast becoming Moravian in doctrine and practice. Bohler, however, soon left for America, and Wesley was not chosen to succeed him.

Count Zinzendorf, the gracious but lordly commander of Moravianism, sent instead a man from Germany, Philip Henry Molther. Molther assumed that most members of the Society were not truly converted and, stressing the Stillness Teaching, advocated waiting in quietness till God should plant faith within them. He suggested also that they refrain from partaking of the Sacrament of the Church of England lest they trust in it for salvation.

Some of the people, however, carried this teaching to an extreme. They refused even to attend the services of the Church of England, and a few went so far as to declare they no longer believed in doing good works, lest these also be depended upon to save them.

To Wesley this attitude was a denial of the function of the Church, and in the meetings of the Society he contended against it. In his striving he exaggerated these tendencies and charged that they characterized the entire Moravian movement. He finally led nineteen people out of the Fetter Lane hall and into a Society he had recently formed in a building he termed the Foundery. Thus he also removed himself from being subject to the superior rank of Count Zinzendorf.

Wesley next separated from Whitefield. Upon leaving Bristol Whitefield had "conjured" him, said Wesley, "to enter into no disputes, least of all concerning Predestination. . . ."[1] Predestination is a doctrine essential to "Calvinism," a theological system he knew Whitefield favored. But Wesley had been taught, particularly by his mother, to believe the opposite system, known as "Arminianism."

A recent development, however, made Whitefield's counsel, "enter into no disputes," difficult for Wesley to follow. Under Wesley's ministry people had begun to undergo convulsion-like attacks, causing them to lie on the ground writhing, and he reports instances in which four strong men could not hold one who was subject to this experience. Charles Wesley spoke of the experience as "the fits," and Whitefield also expressed his dislike of it. These inexplicable events took place only under John Wesley's ministry, and he was certain that they were supernatural signs which God was effecting through him alone.

Thus far Wesley's position in the evangelistic work was secondary. Whitefield had the great congregations; he had begun the open-air ministry and had thrust Wesley into undertaking it too. But Wesley possessed inherited traits that made it natural for him to desire the prime position, and it was this ability that God later used in making him the leader that he became. But as Robert Southey stated, "If he was incapable of bearing with an equal, Wesley could as little brook a superior,"[2] and it was not surprising that he would seek to make himself superior to Whitefield, as he had to Count Zinzendorf and as he would later to Lady Huntingdon.

Accordingly, convinced by the "supernatural" experiences that he no longer needed to remain secondary to Whitefield, he prepared a sermon "against Predestination." But wanting further evidence that his doctrine was true, he cast a lot to obtain it. The lot indicated, "Preach and Print," and therefore he preached the sermon. It had been exactly four weeks from the day Whitefield had introduced him to his Bristol congregation and had "conjured" him not to do the very thing he was now doing.

In the sermon, which he termed "Free Grace,"[3] Wesley began by defining predestination. He did not state some recognized definition, but gave it a meaning of his own, and then declared that all who hold the doctrine must hold it in the same extreme sense. He then went on to assert concerning predestination,

> It is a doctrine full of blasphemy, of such blasphemy as I should dread to mention, but the honour of our gracious God and the cause of truth, will not suffer me to be silent. . . . I will mention a few of the horrible blasphemies contained in this horrible doctrine.
>
> This doctrine represents our blessed Lord, 'Jesus Christ the righteous' as an hypocrite, a deceiver of the people, a man void of common sincerity.
>
> This is the blasphemy clearly contained in the horrible decree of predestination! And here I fix my foot. On this I join issue with every assertor of it. You represent God as worse than the devil; more false, more cruel, more unjust. . . .

Having made these assertions, Wesley adopted for the sake of argument a position in which he supposed the doctrine of predestination to be true, and from that position he thus addressed the Devil:

> Thou fool, why dost thou roar about any longer? Thy lying in wait for souls is as needless and useless as our preaching. Hearest thou not that God hath taken thy work out of thy hands; and that He doeth it more effectively? Thou, with all thy principalities and powers canst only assault that we may resist thee; but He can irresistibly destroy both body and soul in hell!
>
> O how would the enemy of God and man rejoice to hear these things were so! How would he cry aloud and spare not! How would he lift up his voice and say, 'To your tents, O Israel! Flee from the face of this God, or ye shall utterly perish!' But whither will ye flee? Into heaven? He is there. Down to hell? He is there also. Ye cannot flee from an omnipresent tyrant. . . .

We do Wesley no wrong in assessing his motives in separating from the Moravians and from Whitefield. He definitely believed the Moravians were at fault in their failure to use the Sacrament of the Church of England; and even though he had not correctly understood Calvinism, he was sincerely certain it was erroneous. But he also possessed a sense of his own superiority and a mighty ambition, and these tendencies were basic to his actions.

Wesley shortly went to London, and Whitefield had him preach immediately to a great audience. "The Lord give him ten thousand times more success than He has given me,"[4] he prayed, and he went on to have him preach also to his Moorfields and Kennington congregations.

Wesley returned to Bristol, but when Whitefield heard of his sermon he wrote to him saying, "I hear, Honoured Sir, that you are about to print a sermon against predestination. It shocks me to think of it! What will be the consequences but controversy? . . . Silence on both sides will be best."[5]

However, in his declaration, "Here I fix my foot! On this I join issue with every assertor of it!" Wesley had vowed contention. The lot had said, "Preach and Print," and it would not be long before he sent this divisive sermon throughout the land.

Wesley now began also to declare a still more divisive doctrine, that which he termed "Christian Perfection."[6]

He did not, however, clearly define this teaching. Rather he left it in two forms, and they were contradictory. It could mean merely a high state of Christian maturity, and, of course, on this definition there was no difference of opinion. But it could also mean a state of entire sinlessness, and concerning this the strongest of differences existed. Yet it was this latter meaning that Wesley constantly presented, and this was the doctrine's only *raison d'etre*.

Whitefield heard various of Wesley's followers claim that they were perfect, declaring they had not sinned in so many weeks or months, and to him the assertion was both un-Scriptural and dangerous.

Personal holiness was an important element of Whitefield's daily life. Statements to this effect abound in his letters and sermons, and he summed up his attitude in saying,

> Every grace that is in the blessed Jesus is to be transplanted into our hearts; we are to be delivered from the power of sin but not from the indwelling and being of sin in this life. *Hereafter* we are to be preserved blameless, without spot or wrinkle, or any such thing.

Howell Harris's views in this matter agreed entirely with those of Whitefield, and during these days Harris exhorted a friend,

> Rest not till you have the Spirit of God continually bearing witness with your spirit that you are born of God; . . . see that faith grows, and then

Love, Meekness, Brokenness of heart, Godly sorrow, Resignation of will, Humility, Holy fear, watchfulness, tenderness of conscience, and all other graces will grow.

These doctrinal differences enabled Wesley to begin a cause of his own — his own branch of Methodism. He erected a small building at Bristol, the New Room, and had Whitefield come and join together the two main Societies. Using it as his Bristol meeting-place, he termed his movement "The United Societies." As we have seen, he also acquired a building in London, the Foundery, and this he made his headquarters. Though Charles opposed the convulsion experiences, he agreed with John on other matters, and together they pursued their cause with unremitting zeal.

During these months Whitefield entered into a friendship with a young lady, Elizabeth Delamotte. Her father, Thomas Delamotte, was the master of a grand mansion, Blendon Hall, at Bexley, a few miles southeast of London. Thomas also operated a sugar-importing business in London, and while there he and members of his family attended the Fetter Lane Society. Elizabeth and her sister had professed conversion under the influence of Charles Wesley, and the home frequently resounded with the singing of hymns and the voice of prayer.

Whitefield was then expecting at any time to board the vessel that would carry him to America, and he needed to be near the downriver ports. Thus, at Thomas's invitation he became a guest at Blendon Hall, but ranged out daily on his ministry. He had never allowed himself a close friendship with any member of the opposite sex, but now, although he fought against the tendency, he found an affection for Elizabeth forcing itself into his heart.

As the time of his departure drew near, knowing that he would be out of England for a year or more, Whitefield overlooked Wesley's divisive actions and informed his numerous followers in Bristol, Gloucester, and London that Wesley would lead them during his absence. Then, on Monday, August 13, 1739, he dined with the Delamottes, of whom he speaks as "my dear weeping friends," and they accompanied him to Gravesend where his vessel was ready to sail.

Thus, with these two matters upon his mind — his dread of the division being caused by Wesley and his affection for Elizabeth Delamotte — Whitefield set out on his second visit to America.

The whole world is now my parish. Wheresoever my Master calls me I am ready to go and preach the everlasting Gospel.

(Whitefield made this statement while on his voyage to America in 1739. And he made it again nearly thirty years later — not long before his death. And between the two, with his lifetime of labor — seven visits to America, fifteen to Scotland, two to Ireland, one each to Gibraltar, Bermuda, and Holland, together with attempts to reach Canada and the West Indies, preaching to uncounted numbers of mankind — he endeavored mightily to fulfill his declaration.)

7

Doctrinal Convictions

*W*hile crossing the ocean Whitefield no longer had, of course, his vast congregations to whom he could preach. Accordingly, he sought to promote the work of God by the one means available — his correspondence. He wrote a large number of letters, and we will examine a brief selection of them.

To an English clergyman he stated, "As the Lord has been pleased to reveal his dear Son in us, O let us stir up the gift of God and with all boldness preach him to others. . . . What Christ tells us by his Spirit in our closets let us proclaim upon the housetops. All the devils in hell will not be able to hurt us till we have finished our testimony."[1]

Before leaving England he had addressed the students at Philip Doddridge's Academy, a non-Anglican school for training ministers, and now he wrote, ". . . whether Conformists or Nonconformists, our main concern should be to be assured that we are called and taught of God. . . . I thought that most of you were bowed down too much with the servile fear of man. . . . Unless your hearts are free from worldly hopes and worldly fears you will never speak boldly as you ought to speak."[2]

Moreover, in these letters there appear statements in which Whitefield declares again his concept of the responsibility borne by any man in the ministry and of the work that he felt God was about to do on the earth. We notice the following two:

I love those that thunder out the Word. The Christian world is in a deep sleep! Nothing but a loud voice can awaken them out of it.[3]

Oh for a revival of true and undefiled religion in all sects whatsoever! God make me an instrument in promoting it! Methinks I care not what I do or suffer, so that I may see my Lord's kingdom come with power.[4]

Nevertheless, despite the sense of joy and relaxation that first characterized the letters Whitefield wrote on board, into his correspondence there began to come statements of a very different nature.
Saying, "I had a glorious opportunity of spending many hours in
close communion with God, to ask pardon for the defects of my public ministry," he went on to conduct a severe self-examination. He
was led first to a new vision of the unapproachable heights of divine
holiness, and then, in contrast, to a new sight of human sin: the darkness of sin as it appears in the sight of God, sin as it exists in fallen
human nature, and above all sin as it dwelt within his own heart.

In this experience Whitefield was brought very low. At one point
he felt he ought to relinquish the ministry: "A sense of unworthiness
and unfitness so weighs me down that I have often thought it would
be best for me to retire." He even went so far as to suggest he should
refrain from further correspondence: "I feel myself so wretched and
miserable, so blind and naked, that Satan would tempt me to write to
no one." As he anticipated appearing before the public again he
asked, "Must I venture myself once more among fire-brands, arrows
and death?" Yet he finally answered his question with the assertion,
"Yes, if I come forth in the strength of the Lord!" A critic in London
had spoken of him as "Crazy, confident Whitefield!" Yet it is evident
that this youth had little confidence in himself, but rather found his
strength in the Lord his God.

But as God thus gave Whitefield to see something deeper of the
nature of sin, even more did He give him to understand in a new and
fuller measure the exceeding riches of His grace. In several letters he
links the two experiences together, as in the following statements:

A sense of my actual sins and natural deformity humbled me exceedingly; and then the freeness and riches of God's everlasting love broke
in with such light and power upon my soul, that I was often awed into
silence and could not speak![5]

This latter part of the week, blessed be the Lord, He has restored me to
the light of His countenance, and enabled me to praise Him with joyful
lips.

In view of this deeper understanding of divine grace, Whitefield
began to tell forth in his letters the truths he had experienced. In doing

so he enunciated the principles of the theological system he had been embracing — the system usually called "Calvinism," but which he preferred to term "the doctrines of grace."

Whitefield's beliefs, however, were not mere intellectual theories. Rather, they were the basic truths that molded his thought and governed his daily life, and he declared them in letter after letter during this crossing of the ocean. The following two quotations give a general statement of his views:

> This, however, is my comfort.'Jesus Christ saw me from eternity; He gave me being; He called me in time; He has freely justified me through faith in His blood; He has in part sanctified me by His Spirit; He will preserve me underneath His everlasting arms till time shall be no more.' Oh the blessedness of these evangelical truths! These are indeed Gospel; they are glad tidings of great joy to all that have ears to hear.[6]

> Satan will accuse me; my answer shall be, The Lord Jesus is my righteousness; how darest thou to lay anything to the charge of God's elect? I stand here, not in my own, but His robes; and though I deserve nothing as a debt, yet I know He will give me a reward of grace, and recompence me for what He has done in me and by me, as though I had done it in my own power. Oh, how ought this to excite our zeal and love for the holy Jesus![7]

Whitefield declared he had learned these truths from the Scriptures. "I embrace the Calvinistic scheme," he wrote, "not because Calvin, but Jesus Christ has taught it to me." He counseled his friend James Hervey (a man who became very prominent as an author), "Let me advise dear Mr Hervey, laying aside all prejudice, to read and pray over St Paul's epistles to the Romans and Galatians, and then let him tell me what he thinks of this doctrine."

Whitefield declared that these truths were the source of his zeal. To one man he wrote,

> The doctrines of our election and free justification in Christ Jesus . . . fill my soul with a holy fire and afford me great confidence in God my Saviour.
>
> I hope we shall catch fire from each other [he said to another], and that there shall be a holy emulation amongst us who shall most debase

man and exalt the Lord Jesus. Nothing but the doctrines of the Reformation can do this. All others leave free will in man and make him, in part at least, a Saviour to himself. My soul, come thou not near the secret of those who teach such things. . . . I know Christ is all in all. Man is nothing: he hath a free will to go to hell, but none to go to heaven, till God worketh in him to will and do of His good pleasure.[8]

To Whitefield the doctrines of grace were not separate tenets to be accepted or rejected one by one. Rather, they were so joined together as to compose a unified system of theology. In this regard he stated,

I bless God His Spirit has convinced me of our eternal election by the Father through the Son, of our free justification through faith in His blood, of our sanctification as a consequence of that, and of our final perseverance and glorification as the result of all. These I am persuaded, God has joined together; these, neither men nor devils shall ever be able to put asunder.[9]

He also said,

Was there any fitness foreseen in us, except a fitness for damnation? I believe not. No, God chose us from eternity, He called us in time, and I am persuaded will keep us from falling finally, till time shall be no more. Consider the Gospel in this view and it appears a consistent scheme.

Finally, Whitefield looked upon these doctrines as the foundation of a most fervent, soul-winning ministry. When writing to Howell Harris he stated,

Put them in mind of the freeness and eternity of God's electing love, and be instant with them to lay hold of the perfect righteousness of Jesus Christ by faith. Talk to them, oh talk to them, even till midnight, of the riches of His all-sufficient grace. Tell them, oh tell them, what He has done for their souls, and how earnestly He is now interceding for them in heaven. Shew them, in the map of the Word, the kingdoms of the upper world, and the transcendent glories of them; and assure them all shall be theirs if they believe on Jesus Christ with their whole hearts.
Press them to believe on Him immediately! Intersperse prayers with

your exhortations, and thereby call down fire from heaven, even the fire of the Holy Ghost. . . . Speak every time, my dear brother, as if it were your last. Weep out, if possible, every argument, and as it were, compel them to cry, 'Behold how he loveth us!'[10]

In the lack of accuracy that has characterized so much that has been written about Whitefield, it has been stated that he was not a Calvinist until he came under the influence of men in New England and that he had little understanding of what he believed. Thus it must be emphasized that it was before he ever met the New England ministers that he made the above declarations. Moreover, he had gradually come into these convictions over the four years since his conversion, and he possessed a very real understanding of them, not as an abstract system of thought, but as the teachings of the Scriptures and as the basic principles of his daily life.

In these experiences while crossing the ocean, God had further prepared His servant for the extraordinary labor that lay before him.

After eleven weeks of sailing, the vessel reached Lewistown in America. The date was October 30, 1739, and Whitefield was twenty-four.

(Whitefield laid the foundations of Methodism in America. The Wesleys were there but once and then only in the wilderness Colony of Georgia, Charles remaining seven months and John twenty-two. Whitefield made seven visits of various lengths to America and preached repeatedly throughout its thirteen Colonies. And this visit of 1740, which witnessed the Great Awakening, was undoubtedly the richest time of spiritual blessing in the nation's history.)

8

The House of Mercy

*W*hitefield had set out for Pennsylvania, the geographic center of the Colonies. He intended to build an Orphan House in Georgia, but he wanted, as preparation, to obtain a knowledge of America.

Reaching Philadelphia, he was immediately welcomed by the Presbyterian and Baptist pastors and by Thomas Penn, the one remaining member of the founding family. He preached each evening to tremendous crowds in the open air and stated, "They did not seem weary of standing, nor was I weary of speaking." It was evident that the popularity which had been his in England was to be his here also.

Whitefield soon manifested, however, his willingness to sacrifice popular acclaim for Scriptural truth. A prominent Presbyterian pastor, the Rev. William Tennent, paid him a visit. Claiming that a widespread departure from Biblical truth had long been evident in the Presbyterian body, Tennent had "earnestly contended for the faith" in denominational gatherings. But he had also founded a school, commonly known as the Log College, for the training of men for the ministry, and his own scholarship and personal fervor enabled him to equip them with thorough learning and a fiery zeal. Whitefield said,

> He and his sons are secretly despised by the generality of the Synod, as Mr Erskine and his brethren are hated by the judicatories of Edinburgh, and as the Methodist preachers are by their brethren in England.[1]

The controversy on these matters was already dividing not only the Presbyterian but also the Baptist, Reformed, and Congregational bodies, and Whitefield now extended it into his own denomination, the Church of England. Concerning his Sunday afternoon meeting he said, "I was much carried out in bearing my testimony against the unchristian principles and practices of our clergy. Three of my reverent brethren were present. . . . I endeavoured to speak with meekness, as well as zeal."

Whitefield now commenced two important acquaintances. One was with Thomas Noble of New York, a man of considerable possessions who had written indicating his intention of assisting in the establishment of the Orphan House and asking Whitefield to visit him. The other was with William Tennent's son Gilbert, a zealous preacher who accompanied him on this journey.

After returning from New York, Whitefield conducted his ministry in the largest church in Philadelphia and then, finding it too small, resorted to the open air.

William Seward, knowing that a vessel would be highly serviceable to the Orphan House, purchased a sloop and named it *The Savannah*. The party Whitefield had brought from England then set sail for Georgia. But Whitefield, desiring to learn more about America, set out, accompanied by Seward and Whitefield's secretary John Syms, to make the journey by land.

As Whitefield expected, the journey afforded him valuable experience. He preached daily to crowds when in populated areas and to handfuls in wilderness places. The three men were nearly drowned while crossing the Potomac. Although accommodated at times in grand homes, they usually slept in cabins or on the ground. Whitefield expressed his delight in visiting William and Mary College and remarked that two of the professors had been his contemporaries at Oxford. He met numerous people and saw several plantations and noticed especially their dependence on the labor of slaves.

When Whitefield reached Savannah, he found a letter from Elizabeth Delamotte awaiting him. He had felt that he could not truly love God if he allowed himself to love a woman, and since leaving England he had told himself that he had put her out of his mind. But the letter reawakened his affection, and he was thrust into his inward strife again.

The trustees of Georgia had granted Whitefield five hundred acres of land, and he shortly began the construction of the Orphan House. Besides the large central structure, there were to be four smaller buildings. More land had to be cleared, a barn and a dock built, and a road cut throughout the ten miles from Savannah. He hired every available man in the Colony, and all this work looked to him for the energy to see that it was done and for the money to pay for it.

He called the Orphan House "Bethesda," a Biblical term meaning "A House of Mercy."

The need was so evident that Whitefield could not wait for construction to be completed. So he rented the largest house in Savannah and filled it with orphaned children. Not only did he provide them with a home, but they were likewise given schooling and training in obedience and Christian principles. The girls also learned weaving and sewing, and the boys were taught carpentry and farming.

While Bethesda was being built, Whitefield set out on what we may call his Spring Evangelistic Tour. He traveled first to Philadelphia aboard the sloop, taking with him a company of Moravians. These people had refused to bear arms in defending Georgia, and since they wished to remove to Pennsylvania and were poor, Whitefield gave them free passage.

While on the sloop sailing towards Philadelphia, Whitefield made one of the most important decisions of his life. He wrote to Elizabeth Delamotte proposing marriage.

He had already replied to the letter he received from her at Savannah, telling her in his first paragraph, "There is nothing I dread more than having my heart drawn away by earthly objects. When that time comes it will be over with me. . . ."[2] But in his last paragraph he had revealed that he longed to be with her again in England.

Aboard the sloop he wrote to her parents asking their permission to propose marriage to their daughter and enclosing a second letter that he suggested, if satisfied, they give to her. In the letter for her he listed the sacrifices she could be called upon to make in marrying him and the trials she would endure, and then he stated,

> If after seeking to God for direction . . . you can say, 'I can do all those things through Christ strengthening me,' what if you and I were joined together in the Lord, and you came with me at my return from England, to be an help meet to me in the management of the Orphan House. . . . I make no great profession to you. . . . The passionate expressions which carnal courtiers use, I think ought to be avoided by those that would marry in the Lord. . . . I trust I love you only for God. . . . With fear and much trembling I write, and shall patiently tarry my Lord's leisure, till he is pleased to incline you, dear Miss, to send an answer to,

Your affectionate brother, friend and servant in Christ. G.W.[3]

Upon reaching Philadelphia Whitefield sent these letters on their way, and he began the four months' wait necessary in those days for trans-Atlantic correspondence. His soul would be burdened with concern till he received an answer, a condition we must bear in mind as we consider his next months of activity. We may be tempted to smile at him as a lover, but his sincerity is evident in every line he wrote.

At Philadelphia Whitefield entered into an extraordinary friendship, one that continued throughout his life. It was with America's philosopher-statesman, Benjamin Franklin. Years later Franklin looked back and reported,

In 1739 there arrived among us the Rev Mr Whitefield. The multitude of all sects and denominations that attended his sermons was enormous, and it was a matter of speculation with me, who was one of their number, to observe the extraordinary influence of his oratory on his hearers.

It was wonderful to see the change soon made in the manners of our inhabitants. From being thoughtless or indifferent about religion, it seemed as if all the world were growing religious, so that one could not walk thro' the town in an evening without hearing psalms sung in different families in every street.

He had a loud and clear voice, and articulated his words and sentences so perfectly, that he might be heard and understood at a great distance, especially as his audiences, however numerous, observed the most exact silence. He preached one evening from the top of the Court House steps, which are in the middle of Market street, and on the west side of Second-street, which crosses it at right angles. Both streets were filled with his hearers to a considerable distance. Being among the hindmost in Market-street, I had the curiosity to learn how far he could be heard, by retiring backwards down the street towards the river; and I found his voice distinct till I came near Front-street, when some noise in that street obscured it. Imagining then a semi-circle, of which my distance should be the radius, and that it were filled with auditors, to each of whom I allowed two square feet, I computed that he might well be heard by more than thirty thousand. . . . [4]

Franklin has left a striking testimony regarding Whitefield's persuasive powers in pleading for the Orphan House. He says,

Mr Whitefield . . . made large collections, for his eloquence had a wonderful power over the hearts and purses of his hearers, of which I myself was an instance.

I did not disapprove of the design, but as Georgia was then destitute of workmen and materials, and it was proposed to send them from Philadelphia at great expense, I thought it would have been better to have built the house here and brought the children to it. . . .

I happened, soon after, to attend one of his sermons, in the course of which I perceived he intended to finish with a collection, and I silently resolved he should get nothing from me. I had in my pocket a handful of copper, three or four silver dollars and five pistoles in gold. As he proceeded I began to soften and concluded to give the coppers. Another stroke of his oratory made me ashamed of that, and I determined to give the silver; and he finished so admirably that I emptied my pocket wholly into the collector's dish, gold and all.

At this sermon there was also one of our club, who, being of my sentiments respecting the building in Georgia, and suspecting a collection might be intended had by precaution emptied his pockets before he came from home. Towards the conclusion of the discourse, however, he felt a strong desire to give, and applied to a neighbour who stood near him, to borrow some money for the purpose. The application was unfortunately made, to perhaps the only man in the company who had the firmness not to be affected by the preacher. His answer was, 'At any other time, Friend Hopkinson, I would lend thee freely; but not now, for thou seems to be out of thy right senses.'[5]

Franklin became Whitefield's chief American publisher, and he and various members of the Franklin family regarded Whitefield as a personal friend. We shall notice some of the letters that passed between these two men. It is a sad error that their relationship has not been accorded a place in the common concept of the life of each.

Being used to the milder English weather, Whitefield found the heat in America hard to bear. His first biographer, Dr. Gillies of Glasgow, says that during these weeks, "Sometimes he was almost dead with heat and fatigue. Thrice a day he was lifted upon his horse, unable to mount otherwise; then rode and preached, and came in and laid himself along two or three chairs." But no matter how weary he might be, to stand before a crowd and face the responsibility of declaring the gospel had a reviving effect upon him. For the hour — or perhaps two — of intense activity of mind and body he became incredibly strong, till the immense task was completed and he sank into exhaustion again.

This physical exhaustion was undoubtedly increased by two burdens on his mind. One was his concern as to the outcome of his proposal of marriage, and the other was the disharmony John Wesley was creating in England. At Philadelphia he received a letter from Wesley, and he replied,

> The more I examine the writings of the most experienced men and the experiences of the most established Christians, the more I differ from your notion of not committing sin, and your denying the doctrines of election and final perseverance. . . .
>
> I dread coming to England unless you are resolved to oppose these truths with less warmth than when I was there last. I dread your coming over to America; because the work of God is carried on here (and that in a most glorious manner) by doctrines quite opposite to those you hold. . . . God direct me what to do. Sometimes I think it best to stay here, where we all think and speak the same thing. The work goes on without divisions. . . .
>
> I write not this, Honoured Sir, from heat of spirit, but out of love. From my soul I wish you abundant success. . . . I long to hear of your being made a spiritual father to thousands. . . . Do not be angry with, but pray for, Honoured Sir,
>
> Your unworthy brother and servant in Christ, G.W.[6]

Knowing that men in general, in expressing their differences of opinion, may become harsh with one another, certain authors have assumed that Whitefield must have been uncivil towards Wesley. But the true nature of his spirit — peace-seeking and loving — is evident in this letter, as in all his letters to Wesley, and is fully expressed in Charles Wesley's *Elegy on Whitefield*.

Whitefield's inherent kindness is manifest also in an action he now undertook to assist the black men and women in America. Having witnessed the cruelty practiced on many slaves, he now wrote and published *A Letter to the Inhabitants of Maryland, Virginia, and North and South Carolina Concerning Their Negroes*. It read, in part,

Your dogs are caressed and fondled at your tables, but your slaves, who are frequently styled dogs or beasts, have not an equal privilege. They are scarce permitted to pick up the crumbs that fall from their masters' tables. Nay, some . . . have been, upon the most trifling provocation, cut with knives, and have had forks thrown into their flesh; not to mention what numbers have been given up to the inhuman usage of cruel task-masters, who, by their unrelenting scourges, have ploughed upon their backs, and made long furrows, and at length brought them even to death itself. I hope there are few such monsters of barbarity suffered to subsist among you.

Is it not the highest ingratitude as well as cruelty, not to let your poor slaves enjoy some fruits of their labour? Whilst I have viewed your plantations cleared and cultivated, and have seen many spacious houses, and the owners of them faring sumptuously every day, my blood has almost run cold within me, when I have considered how many of your slaves have neither convenient food to eat, nor proper raiment to put on, notwithstanding most of the comforts you enjoy were solely owing to their indefatigable labours. . . . 'Go to, ye rich men, weep and howl, for your miseries shall come upon you!' Behold the provision of the poor negroes, which have reaped your fields, which is by you denied them, crieth, and the cries of them which have reaped have come into the ears of the Lord of Saboth![7]

This letter, which sounded as though it were a declaration by an Old Testament prophet, received a speedy circulation. Whitefield gave it to Franklin to be published in pamphlet form, but it was also reprinted in newspapers in almost all the Colonies.

Whitefield also attempted to assist the slaves in a material way. In his *Journal* he wrote, "This day I bought five thousand acres of land on the forks of the Delaware, and ordered a large house to be built thereupon for the instruction of these poor creatures." He called the proposed institution by the Biblical name "Nazareth."

The party of Moravians that Whitefield had brought from Georgia was under the direction of Peter Bohler, the man who had been influential in the conversion of Charles and John Wesley. It was composed of only three other men, besides two women and two boys; but since they were homeless and in need of work, Whitefield offered to employ them in constructing the Nazareth house. After casting a lot they journeyed to the site, some forty miles from Philadelphia.

Although completely in the wilderness and surrounded by hostile Indians, they began the building immediately.

As Whitefield traversed the Colonies, his relation with the blacks was warm and friendly. His preaching was always simplified so as to be understandable to these people who were almost entirely without schooling. Indeed, he often spoke directly to them while he was preaching. "Did you ever hear of the eunuch belonging to Queen Candace, a negro like yourselves?" he asked in a sermon on "The Lord Our Righteousness." "He believed. The Lord was his righteousness. Do you also believe, and you shall be saved."

Whitefield preached extensively throughout the Middle Colonies, and he saw not only a multitude of whites, but also many blacks converted. For instance, during his days in Philadelphia he reported, "Nearly fifty negroes came to my lodgings to give thanks for what God had done for their souls." And of his experience during a period of grave sickness he said, "The poor negroes crowded round the windows, and expressed a great concern for me. Their master had acquainted them that I was their friend."

But Nazareth failed to come to the fruition Whitefield had expected. He was never at Nazareth, and he left its affairs to a committee in Philadelphia. The building he had planned was an extensive one, three stories in height and constructed of massive stone. Bohler brought other men from Germantown, but after five months of labor he realized the roof could not be put on before Winter. He began a small log house alongside to provide a place for himself and his party and set out to find Whitefield and inform him of the change.

Since Bohler had but partly learned English and Whitefield spoke no German, they conversed in Latin. Whitefield had been informed by Wesley of "the Stillness Doctrine" and of the refusal of the Moravians to attend the Eucharist of the Church of England, and he agreed with Wesley's stand. Using the ancient language, he and Bohler discussed the matter, and he remarked, ". . . it is best to carry on the work of God apart. . . . God grant that we may keep up a cordial undissembled love towards one another, notwithstanding our different opinions."[8]

Whitefield maintained gracious relations with the Moravians, and the friendship was so warm that before long it was reported that he had become a Moravian himself. Yet, strange as it may seem, the statement has been published and widely believed that "he proved so heartless that he drove Bohler and his party, men, women and children, off his property in the midst of winter."

It proved impossible, however, for Whitefield to complete the construction of the Nazareth building. The Indians round about were openly hostile, and above all, the project was too large for Whitefield financially. The Moravians obtained the property and finished the building, and it stands today as a Moravian museum and as a home for their missionaries while on furlough.

But although Whitefield failed in his endeavor to assist the blacks, he succeeded in other regards. Most important was the effect of his preaching on the creation of the Negro Spiritual. The black man heard from Whitefield spiritual truths declared in a manner that, despite his uneducated condition, he could understand, and he returned to his toil soothing his soul in the truths he had learned. He repeated over and over some phrase he had gained from the lips of the preacher till the repetition became rhythmic and his natively musical soul linked it with melody. He sang it again and again, others heard and joined their voices, and the whole was repeated day after day till it became part and parcel of their lives. Thus was born the heartfelt singing of Scriptural truths by the black man — the Negro Spiritual.

In those days it was frequently asked, "Does the Negro have a soul?" and Whitefield gave the first widely-heard positive reply that the black man was basically no different from the white man. Nevertheless, we cannot but regret that he did not come to the conviction that slavery was utterly evil and demand in his powerful eloquence that "liberty and justice" be granted to all men, black as well as white.

The apostolical times seem to have returned upon us; such a display has there been of the power and grace of the divine Spirit in the assemblies of his people, and such testimonies has he given to the word of the Gospel.

William Cooper
Boston
November 1741

9

Laboring in the Great Awakening

S ome critics have assumed that Whitefield's ministry was conducted without any planning and that he went hither and yon
directed only by his whims. A little knowledge of his life, however, proves the very opposite, and the order and arrangement of his
journeyings is especially manifest in this year in America.

Using Savannah as his base he ranged out, first performing the
labor in the Middle Colonies that we have just seen — the Spring Tour.
Then followed his ministry in and around Charleston — the Summer
Tour, and finally the Fall Tour, in which he preached first in New
England and then all the way back to Georgia. It was a wisely-
planned year of labor which enabled him to effectively reach the populated areas of America.

While Whitefield had been preaching in the Middle Colonies, a
series of strong attacks had been made on him by Commissary
Garden of St. Philip's Church, Charleston. A commissary was com-
missioned by a bishop to act in his place, and Garden was prepared
to exercise all possible authority.

Whitefield's un-Anglican actions (i.e., his refusal to conform to the
parish system ordained by the Church, and his preaching for men of
other denominations) had already aroused Garden's ire. Garden was
equally repulsed by Whitefield's *Letter to the Slave Owners*, and to
this was now added another, *A Letter to Archbishop Tillotson*, in
which Whitefield declared that "the Archbishop knew no more of
true Christianity than Mahomet." In turn, Commissary Garden leaped
into action and published *Six Letters to the Rev George Whitefield*,
and in these he revealed his outrage.

It should be explained that although Archbishop Tillotson had been dead for nearly half a century, his memory was highly regarded and his writings were still widely-read. But Whitefield had become aroused by the statement of a wealthy planter, Hugh Bryan, that he had been kept for years in darkness through reading the archbishop, and therefore the evangelist made his strong statement.

Charleston contained numerous citizens who stood strongly in favor of the Tillotsonian vogue in religion. The city was also a commercial center for many planters whose wealth was derived from the labor of the slave. Accordingly, a great number of men and women were violently angry on account of Whitefield's two *Letters*, and Commissary Garden, in his *Six Letters* to Whitefield, sought to make himself spokesman for their hostility, as well as his own.

Garden's thought and manner are evident in the following excerpts: "Alas! the fire you have kindled is that of slander and defamation, — a fire which no devil in hell, nor Jesuit on earth, will ever go about to extinguish, but will fagot and foment it with all their might, as too effectively serving their interests." "In your mountebank way you have David-like, as you fancy, slain your Goliath [Tillotson] but his works and memory will long survive after you and your dirty pamphlets are sunk into oblivion." He declared that the slaveowners should sue Whitefield for slander, and he sought to make a mockery of Whitefield's charges of cruelty to the slaves by asserting, "I have heard the report of your cruelty to the poor orphans under your care, not only in pinching their bellies, but in giving them up to taskmasters or mistresses who plow upon their backs and make long furrows in a very inhuman manner."[1]

Whitefield made no reply to Garden's *Letters*, but his cause was taken up by Rev. Josiah Smith, minister of Charleston's Independent Church. Smith preached a sermon entitled "The Character, Preaching, Etc., of the Rev Mr Whitefield," and it was published, including a recommendatory preface by two prominent New England ministers, Cooper and Colman. These widely-esteemed men said of Whitefield,

... he is the wonder of the age; and no man more employs the pens and fills the conversation of people, than he does ... none more admired and applauded by some, condemned and reproached by others.[2]

Smith opened his sermon with the assertion that Whitefield's preaching was always doctrinal, and he listed the doctrines the evangelist proclaimed. Then he went on to state,

> I need not say, nor can my pen describe, his action and gesture, in all their strength and decencies. He is certainly a finished preacher, and a great master of pulpit oratory, though a noble negligence runs through his style. His discourses were very extraordinary, when we consider how little they were premeditated, and how many of them he gave us in the little while he was with us. . . .[3]

Smith goes on to speak of Whitefield's holiness of life, his power in prayer, the graciousness of his manner, his selflessness, his diligence, and his charity. "Strolling and vagabond orphans, poor and helpless, without father, without mother, without purse and without friend, he seeks out, picks up and adopts into his family . . . what brighter evidence of pure religion is there than this, 'to visit the fatherless in their affliction!'"

Smith's sermon described a ministry so magnificent that it made Garden's opposition appear trivial and jaundiced. And such was the situation when, at the pressing invitation of numerous citizens, Whitefield arrived at Charleston. The date was July 1740.

In keeping with his custom of attending the Church of England, on the Sunday morning he went as an ordinary worshiper to St. Philip's. Garden delivered a virulent attack against him and then refused him the Sacrament. Whitefield filled the rest of the day and also the following week with preaching.

The next Sunday saw him again at St. Philip's. This time Garden had ransacked church history to find fanatics to whom to liken him, and after mentioning several he produced one that was familiar and repulsive to all. This was the Dutarts, a Charleston family who had practiced weird religious rites, lived as outlaws, and had been guilty of notorious incests and murders. Garden had served as chaplain at their hangings, and it was to these people that he likened Whitefield.[4]

Although no ecclesiastical court had ever been held outside of England, Garden convened one. He intended to utilize his full authority against Whitefield and to expel him from the ministry. Clothed in ecclesiastical splendor, Garden sat as the judge with clergymen on each side. The proceedings were marked by all possible pomp and display of authority. But on the third day of the trial Whitefield seized the initiative, and declared that Garden did not possess the authority to try him. After announcing his appeal to the High Court in Chancery in London, he walked out of the court.

Upon reaching London in the following year (we anticipate our story), he repeatedly attempted to have the High Court consider the matter. But the English judges would not take Garden's petty court seriously, and they refused to hear the case.

But Garden acted. "A year and a day" after convening his court he convened it again. This time, "in a cloud of high-sounding words" he suspended Whitefield from the ministry and "declared him to be denounced . . . openly and publicly in the face of the Church."[5] Whitefield paid not the least attention to Garden's excommunication, except to state, "I pitied, I prayed for him, and wished the Lord would convert him."

Whitefield's experiences in Charleston, however, had a lasting effect upon him. He preached in one or two churches of the Church of England, but it was especially in Presbyterian, Independent, and Baptist churches that he was welcomed. He had warm fellowship with several of their ministers, and from this time forward while in America he increasingly forsook his practice of attending the Church of England on Sunday mornings.

The Baptists of the Southern Colonies in particular benefitted from Whitefield's influence. Baptist churches and Baptist people were few in the South at the time, unbelief was entering among them, and a zeal for soul-winning was rare. But moved by Whitefield's ministry many of these churches became firm in the faith, and a new fervor began to characterize them. They increased in number with great speed as men — many of them farmer-preachers — preached the gospel in tents, in barns, and in the open air. Souls in great numbers were won to Christ.

Moreover, while Whitefield was at Charleston, Commissary Garden confronted him with a copy of Wesley's sermon "Against Predestination."[6] This was Whitefield's first realization that, contrary to his expressed desire, Wesley was circulating this divisive document, and he could see that the day was approaching when it would be necessary for him to write a reply.

And further disappointment awaited him: he received an answer to his proposal of marriage. He merely tells us, "I find from Blendon letters that Miss E — — D — — is in a seeking state only." Apparently either the parents or Elizabeth had written to say that she was not a sufficiently mature Christian to undergo all the trials he had listed. But the Delamottes, with the rest of the Fetter Lane Society, had become Moravians and were now opposed to the Wesleys, and we must suppose to some degree to Whitefield too. Moreover, Elizabeth was now keeping company with another young man, William Holland, the one spoken of as reading from Luther on the evening John Wesley was converted, and within five months Elizabeth and Holland were married. Our hearts go out to Whitefield in this further disappointment, and we feel for him as following his mention of the "Blendon letters" he says, "Just now I have been weeping, and much carried out before the Lord."

In this sense of deep disappointment he returned to Bethesda.

After a few days spent in superintending the work of the Orphan House, Whitefield set out on his Fall Tour — that of New England. He had been invited by the governor and the secretary of Massachusetts, by a number of laymen, and by several ministers.

And now, as always, Boston people thronged to hear him. Civic officials of today would not allow such crowding as was practiced under Whitefield's ministry in the churches. Time after time humanity pressed into the pews, filled the aisles and the stairways, and covered the pulpit area. But in a congregation that had gathered ahead of time at the New South Church and was waiting for Whitefield to arrive, someone broke a board to form a makeshift seat, and a cry went up that the gallery was falling. Immediately the place was in a panic as people rushed to get to the doors, and many fell and were trampled upon. Some even threw themselves out of the windows. Five were killed and several seriously injured.

Whitefield was severely disturbed by the tragedy, but looking to God for help he led the congregation to the Boston Common where he preached on the text, "Go out into the highways and the hedges, and compel them to come in." He continued his ministry, preaching morning and afternoon each day, and each evening he ministered to the crowd that surged into the house in which he lodged. On that Wednesday he preached twice to the students at Harvard College, and on Sunday he took his first collection in New England, receiving nearly £200.

During these days in Boston, Whitefield was shown admiring attention by the Honorable Jonathan Belcher, governor of

Massachusetts. Belcher was a man of large wealth, and his life had been lived after the fashion of the aristocracy of England. But he now urged Whitefield, ". . . do not spare the rulers, any more than ministers, no not the chief of them. . . . Pray, Mr Whitefield, that I may hunger and thirst after righteousness."

As Whitefield went to his farewell service — a great open-air meeting on the Boston Common — the governor drove him in his carriage. The congregation, estimated in a newspaper as twenty-three thousand, was larger than the entire population of the city, and was undoubtedly the largest crowd ever assembled in America till that time. When his ministry was concluded Whitefield declared, "I hope a glorious work is now begun, and that God will raise up some faithful labourers to carry it on."

Thomas Prince, an earnest Boston minister, stated that before Whitefield's arriving, ". . . the general decay of piety seemed to increase among us . . . few came to me in concern about their souls. And so I perceive it was with others. . . . But upon Mr Whitefield's leaving us great numbers were so happily concerned about their souls . . . our assemblies, both on Lectures and Sabbaths, were surprisingly increased."[7] A regular meeting that proved to be always crowded began to be held on Tuesday evenings, "the first stated *evening* Lecture in these parts of the world."

Upon leaving Boston (October 13, 1740) Whitefield came in four days to Northampton, the site of the ministry of the Rev. Jonathan Edwards. Edwards, the eminent pastor whose ministry had already been used of God in sending revival to Northampton, had especially urged him to visit his town. Edwards had written:

Northampton in New-England, Feb 12, 1740.

Rev. Sir.

My request to you is that in your intended journey through New England . . . you would be pleased to visit Northampton. . . . I apprehend, from what I have heard, that you are one that has the blessing of heaven attending you wherever you go, and I have a great desire, if it be the will of God, that such blessing as attends you and your labours may descend on this town. . . .

It has been with refreshment of soul that I have heard of one raised up in the Church of England to revive the mysterious, spiritual, despised and exploded doctrines of the Gospel, and full of a spirit of zeal for the promotion of real, vital piety, whose labours have been attended with such success. Blessed be God that hath done it! who is with you, and helps you, and makes the weapons of your warfare mighty. . . .

I desire that you and Mr. Seward would come directly to my house. I shall account it a great favour and smile of providence to entertain such guests under my roof. . . .

> I am Rev Sir
> Unworthy to be called your fellow labourer,
> Jonathan Edwards[8]

Whitefield's visit to Northampton lasted from Friday afternoon till Sunday evening. He reported,

> Mr Edwards is a solid, excellent Christian, but at present weak in body. I think I have not seen his fellow in all New England. When I came into his pulpit, I found my heart drawn out to talk of scarce anything beside the consolations and privileges of saints, and the plentiful effusion of the Spirit upon believers.[9]

And concerning the Sunday he wrote,

> Preached this morning and good Mr Edwards wept during the whole time. . . . The people were equally affected; and in the afternoon, the power increased yet more.[10]

Mrs. Edwards was also much taken with Whitefield's ministry. She wrote to her brother, the Rev. James Pierrepont of New Haven, stating,

> It is wonderful to see what a spell he casts over an audience by pro-claiming the simplest truths of the Bible. I have see upward of a thou-sand people hang on his words with breathless silence, broken only by an occasional half-suppressed sob. He impresses the ignorant, and not less the educated and refined . . . our mechanics shut up their shops, and the day-labourers throw down their tools to go and hear him preach, and few return unaffected. . . . Many, very many persons in Northampton

date the beginning of new thoughts, new desires, new purposes, and a new life, from the day they heard him preach of Christ. . . .[11]

Loath to part with Whitefield, Edwards accompanied him for the next two days as he rode to East Windsor, the home of his father, the Rev. Timothy Edwards. After preaching to his people Whitefield said, "His wife was as aged, I believe, as himself, and I fancied I was sitting in the house of Zacharias and Elizabeth. I parted from him and his son with regret."

Two days after leaving Edwards, Whitefield came to Middletown. One of his hearers, Nathan Cole, an unlettered farmer, wrote an account which demonstrates how the mere announcement "Whitefield will preach!" brought virtually the whole countryside hurrying to hear him. Cole wrote.

one morning all on a Suding there came a messanger & said mr whitefield is to preach at middletown this morning at 10 o'clock. i was in my field, dropt my tool & run home and throu my house and bad my wife to get ready quick & run to my pastire for my hors with all my might fearing i should be too late to hear him & took up my wife and went forward as fast as I thought ye hors could bear & when my hors began to be out of breth would get down and put my wife on ye saddel and bid her ride as fast as she could and not Stop for me except i bad her & so would run until I was almost out of breth & then mount my hors again. . . .

i saw before me a cloud or fog . . . as i came nearer ye road i heard a noise something like a low rumbling thunder & presently found out it was ye rumbling of horses feet. . . . i could see men and horses slipping along. . . . i found a vacance between two horses to slip in my hors & my wife said law our cloaths will be all spoiled . . . and when we gat down to ye old meeting house there was a great multitude. . . . I looked towards ye great river I see ye fery boats running swift forward and backward — when I see mr whitefield come up upon ye scaffold he looked almost angellical, a young slim slender youth before thousands of people and with a bold undainted countenance & my hearing how god was with him everywhere. . . . it solemnized my mind & put me in a trembling fear . . . for he looked as if he was clothed with authority . . . & a sweet solemnity sat upon his brow. . . . my old foundation was broken up and I see my righteousness would not save me.[12]

While Cole has thus given us an insight into how Whitefield's great congregations were gathered, another hearer has shown how he could use the circumstances of the moment to illustrate the gospel. This hearer, describing one of Whitefield's services in Boston, tells of the approach of a storm as the evangelist began his sermon. "See that emblem of human life," he said as he pointed to a flitting shadow. "It passed for a moment and concealed the brightness of heaven from our view; but it is gone. And where will you be, my hearers, when your lives have passed away like that dark cloud? Oh, my dear friends . . . in a few days we shall all meet at the Judgement-Seat of Christ. We shall form part of that vast assemblage which will gather before His throne."

Whitefield went on to plead with his hearers, directing his words to "false and hollow Christians," then to "rich men," and finally to the "sinner." After urging, "Let not the fires of eternity be kindled against you!," pointing to a flash of lightning he cried, "See there! It is a glance from the angry eye of Jehovah! Hark!" he continued, raising his finger in a listening attitude as the thunder broke in a tremendous crash, "It is the voice of the Almighty as He passed by in His anger!"

> As the sound died, Whitefield covered his face with his hands and fell on his knees, lost in prayer. The storm passed rapidly away, and the sun, bursting forth, threw across the heavens the magnificent arch of peace. Rising and pointing to it the young preacher cried, "Look upon the rainbow, and praise Him who made it. . . . It compasseth the heavens about with glory, and the hands of the Most High have bended it."[13]

Whitefield was asked for permission to publish the sermon, but recognizing that the natural elements were essential to his meaning he replied, "Yes, if you include the lightning and thunder."

During these days, he was still receiving letters from John Wesley. Wesley constantly mentioned the points of difference and sought to provoke Whitefield into disputing about them. In a reply written on September 25, 1740 Whitefield stated,

> I think I have for some time known what it is to have righteousness, peace and joy in the Holy Ghost. These I believe are the privileges of the sons of God: But I cannot say I am free from indwelling sin. . . . I am sorry, honoured Sir, to hear by many letters, that you seem to own

a *sinless perfection* in this life attainable. . . . I do not expect to say indwelling sin is destroyed in me till I bow my head and give up the ghost. I know many abuse this doctrine, and perhaps willfully indulge sin. . . .[14]

This letter reveals Whitefield at his strongest in dealing with Wesley. He stands firmly for his convictions, yet his manner is courteous and the opposite of contentious.

A glaring error, however, has been made in this matter. An Englishman to whom Whitefield refers as "young W —" wrote frequently to Whitefield at this time, constantly disputing with him. He was probably a youth who had been converted in one of Whitefield's Religious Societies in Bristol. Whitefield replied, commencing, "Dear Brother W —, What mean you by disputing in all your letters? May God give you to know yourself, and then you will not plead for absolute perfection or call the doctrine of election a 'doctrine of devils.' . . . Remember you are but a babe in Christ, if so much. Be humble, talk little, think and pray much. . . ."[15]

Whitefield thus gave the young fellow a necessary reprimand. But eighty years later Robert Southey, not taking care to investigate the matter, jumped to the conclusion that this letter was written to Wesley. Although Whitefield had addressed it to "Mr W —, at Bristol" Southey published it as to "Mr Wesley at Bristol," and he went on to charge that Whitefield had acted as though he were superior and had treated Wesley in a mean fashion. Several authors have copied this error from Southey.

Whitefield preached at both Harvard and New Haven (Yale) Colleges, asserting that they were now studying books of a harmful nature and declaring a minister's need to be a converted man. A few weeks later Dr. Colman said of Harvard, "The College is entirely changed. The students are full of God. Many of them appear truly born again. The voice of prayer and praise fills their chambers. . . . I was told that not seven out of a hundred in attendance remain unaffected."

Likewise concerning Yale, Jonathan Edwards reported,

The awakening was . . . for a time very great and general at New Haven; and the College had no small share in it. The students in general became serious, many of them remarkably so. . . . There have been manifestly happy and abiding effects of the impressions then made on many members of that College.

One of the students influenced at Yale was David Brainerd. Like many students, he went to something of an extreme in his attitudes, and he stated of one professor, "He has no more grace than this chair!" For this assertion he was expelled, but notwithstanding this action he went forth into a life of extraordinary usefulness as a missionary to the Indians. It has long been regretted that before his death he ordered the burning of the portion of his *Diary* that reported his experiences during his days at the college.

Upon leaving New England, Whitefield set out for Georgia, preaching as he traveled. In every place he ministered to tremendous congregations, and everywhere the spiritual excitement that had been aroused throughout the Colonies characterized great numbers of people.

On January 16, 1741 he set sail for England. He had been in America for fourteen and a half months, and although, as always, he made no estimate of the number of persons who had professed conversion, the abundance of transformed lives was widely manifest.

After Whitefield left for the homeland, the work in America was carried on by other men. Jonathan Edwards continued to perform his remarkably rich ministry and to give calm counsel in writing and preaching to the whole work of the Awakening. Gilbert Tennent went, as Whitefield had suggested, to Boston where he conducted a ministry of great zeal and power. Numerous pastors, being invited to church after church as evangelists, continued the work that had been commenced, and churches that previous to Whitefield's coming had been merely following a religious schedule were now alive with spiritual fervor. The movement was later termed "The Great Awakening," and despite certain setbacks it remained in power for several years.

John Greenleaf Whittier, in his poem on Whitefield, described his ministry and its effect, saying,

> *So the flood of emotion deep and strong*
> *Troubled the land as it swept along,*
> *But left a result of holier lives,*
> *Tenderer mothers and worthier wives,*

The husband and father whose children fled
  And sad wife wept as his drunken tread
Frightened peace from his roof-tree's shade,
  And a rock of offence his hearthstone made,
In a strength that was not his own began
  To rise from the brute's to the plane of man.
Old friends embraced, long held apart,
  By evil counsel and pride of heart,
And penitence saw through misty tears,
  On the bow of hope on its cloud of fears,
The promise of Heaven's eternal years,
  The peace of God for the world's annoy,
Beauty for ashes, and oil of joy.

My Dear, Dear Brethren,

. . . Why did you throw out that bone of contention? Why did you print that sermon against predestination? . . .

Do you not think, my dear brethren, that I must be as much concerned for truth, or what I think truth, as you? God is my judge. I always was, and I hope I always shall be, desirous that you may be preferred before me. But I must preach the Gospel of Christ, and this I cannot now do without speaking about election. . . .

O my dear brethren, my heart almost bleeds within me! Methinks I would be willing to tarry here on the waters forever, rather than come to England to oppose you.

Whitefield to John and Charles Wesley,
from aboard ship, as it approached England
March 1741

10

Whitefield's Darkest Hour

W e have seen that there already were doctrinal differences between Wesley and Whitefield. When Whitefield returned to England, these differences brought about a separation between them. The truth of this matter is often distorted, for although professed reports of it have frequently been published, almost all are so strongly biased in Wesley's favor that both his and Whitefield's actions are very falsely presented.

Accordingly, as much as both writer and reader may find the subject distasteful, if we are not to let falsehoods continue to cloud a most noble portion of Whitefield's life, we have no choice but to look into this matter. We do so, however, very briefly, noticing merely the chief facts.

One of Whitefield's first activities after reaching London was meeting with his old friend, Charles Wesley. John was out of town at the time. Of course, the doctrinal differences were discussed, and the likelihood of schism was recognized. Whitefield stated, "It would have melted any heart to have heard Mr Charles Wesley and me weeping, after prayer, that if possible the breach might be averted."[1] But Charles was as strongly against the doctrine of election as Whitefield was for it, and as adamant in favor of sinless perfection as Whitefield was opposed to it. Charles refused to have any further cooperation with Whitefield, and accordingly they separated. But we shall rejoice when, ten years later, Charles's doctrinal convictions changed to some extent and he came into a considerable measure of agreement with Whitefield. They then again enjoyed a rich friendship, and this continued until Whitefield was removed from him by death.

On Whitefield's first Sunday in London, a burst of enthusiasm brought some thousands to hear him both at Moorfields and Kennington Common. But the enthusiasm quickly waned, and on the weekdays his congregations numbered merely two or three hundred. Moreover, he saw many of his former hearers rush by with their fingers in their ears, and several of them later informed him this had been Wesley's instruction to them to prevent them from hearing heretical doctrine.

The loss of Whitefield's host of hearers not only curtailed his gospel ministry, but also robbed him of the opportunity to collect for the support of the orphans. Moreover, he had expected that a sum of money would be awaiting him from the sale of the volumes of his sermons, but he found that James Hutton, his publisher, had become a Moravian and refused to sell any literature that did not agree with Moravian teachings.

A particular sorrow arose from the fact that William Seward had died. Some few months earlier, in accompanying Howell Harris as he conducted an open-air meeting in Wales, Seward had suffered a severe physical injury at the hands of a mob. But he soon went out again to another meeting, and as the stones were hurled he shouted, "Better endure this than hell!" In a few days' time his body weakened, and he entered his heavenly home. He has long been spoken of as "The first Methodist martyr."

Seward, however, had recently undertaken another £350 debt in the name of the Orphan House, and not only was Whitefield responsible to pay it, but he was threatened with imprisonment if he failed to do so. His creditors gloated over the opportunity seemingly before them, and he was in constant danger of arrest till in a miraculous manner the money became available. Moreover, although Seward had made himself jointly responsible for the maintenance of Bethesda, he died without making a will, and the whole responsibility fell upon Whitefield.

Whitefield's chief sorrow, however, arose from the opposition of John and Charles Wesley. ". . . Many, very many of my spiritual children," he wrote, "who at my last departure from England would have plucked out their own eyes to have given them to me, are so prejudiced by the dear Messrs. W's dressing up the doctrine of election in such horrible colours, that they will neither hear, see, nor give me the least assistance: Yes, some of them send threatening letters that God will speedily destroy me."[2] Yet he still spoke of ". . . my dear, dear old friends, Messrs. John and Charles Wesley, whom I still love as my own soul."[3]

Nevertheless, Whitefield was not without help. A company of friends began building a large wooden shed in the Moorfields district that would shield his hearers from rain and cold. Since the location was not far from Wesley's Foundery, Whitefield refused it. But being reminded that he had been the first to preach at Moorfields, he came round to using it. Yet he thought of it as merely a temporary structure and therefore termed it "The Tabernacle."

Some friends had begun to publish a weekly paper. It carried news of the ministry of himself and of others of a Calvinistic mind on both sides of the Atlantic. He called it *The Weekly History*.

Whitefield also still faced the question as to whether he should publish in England his reply to Wesley's sermon "Free Grace," or as Wesley termed it "Against Predestination." For nineteen months Wesley had circulated this sermon, and both he and Charles had opposed Whitefield's beliefs in their daily ministries. Numerous people had accepted their teachings, and Whitefield decided he had no choice but to print his reply.

He began by declaring his strong reluctance to publish anything critical of Wesley.

> . . . Jonah could not go with more reluctance against Ninevah than I now take pen in hand to write against you. Was nature to speak I had rather die than do it; and yet if I am faithful to God, and to my own and others' souls I must not stand neuter any longer. . . . Numbers have been misled whom God has been pleased to work upon by my ministry, and a greater number are still calling upon me to show also my opinion. I must then shew that I know no man after the flesh, and that I have no respect of persons, any further than is consistent with my duty to my Lord and Master, Jesus Christ.[4]

In this reply Whitefield makes his arguments clearly, and he is unmovable in his doctrinal convictions. But his attitude towards Wesley is characterized by the respect we have seen in his letters, and to him Wesley is ever "My Honoured Friend" and "Honoured Sir." There is definiteness of statement, but never a harsh word.

One point, however, of Whitefield's reply must have our attention. In publishing the sermon, Wesley inserted a brief introduction stating that he had been moved to preach the sermon by "the strongest conviction, not only that what is here advanced is 'the truth as it is in Jesus,' but also that I am indispensably obliged to declare this truth to all the world."5 Numerous readers of the sermon would believe that since he had been "indispensably obliged" in the matter he surely had received some special commission from God, and that therefore the doctrine he declared must indeed be true. The little introduction was as valuable in enforcing Wesley's teaching as any of his arguments.

Yet the "indispensable obligation" was nothing more than the casting of a lot. That is, he had written out two or three possible courses of actions, each on a separate slip of paper; he had picked up one, and it had read "Preach and Print," and this was his authorization for thrusting such a divisive issue into the revival movement.

Accordingly, in his reply Whitefield pointed out that Wesley's "indispensable obligation" was merely a lot. The issue was a doctrinal matter, not a personal one, and to reveal the role of the casting of a lot was essential to removing the false impression Wesley's statement had made. Moreover, Whitefield stated that on a previous occasion Wesley had been mistaken by casting a lot and suggested that Wesley ought to have been more careful in using the practice.

Moreover, Wesley had seized as his own the New Room at Bristol and the School House at Kingswood — buildings for which Whitefield and Seward had raised virtually all the money. Whitefield wrote to him about the matter, and Wesley replied in a long harsh letter.6 He adopted an attitude that he had done nothing to provoke discord and that Whitefield had begun and continued the strife. This totally false attitude Wesley maintained throughout the rest of his life.

During these days, however, Whitefield was gradually winning back his congregations. Thus Wesley realized he was losing much of the fruit of nineteen months of opposition, and the loss provoked him. He made charges that were distorted and untrue, saying that Whitefield refused to offer him the hand of fellowship and that Whitefield asserted he would everywhere preach against him. We can only recognize Wesley's disappointment as the cause of his statements.

Some of Whitefield's people were indignant that he had been so forgiving to Wesley and had not claimed a share in the New Room and the Kingswood School. But Whitefield replied,

My heart doth not reproach me for my kindness and friendship to those that differ from me. . . . I cannot renounce those precious truths that I have felt the power of and which were taught me not of man, but of God. At the same time I would love all that love the Lord Jesus, though they differ with me in some points. . . . I have not given way to the Moravian Brethren, or to Mr Wesley, or to any whom I thought in error, no not for an hour. But I think it best not to dispute when there is no probability of convincing.[7]

Nevertheless, one cannot but feel sorry that Whitefield did not leave an account of his part in the controversy just as fully as Wesley did of his. But Whitefield left us very little and chose to allow Wesley's statements to remain unchallenged. Accordingly, a false concept of the separation and of the actions of its two chief participants has been passed down to mankind, and has become so fixed in the minds of men that any attempt to correct it will undoubtedly seem to many to be biased against Wesley and severely slanted in Whitefield's favor.

Ten years later, however, having occasion then to recall the treatment he had experienced at the hands of the two Wesleys, in a letter to Lady Huntingdon Whitefield stated:

It is good for me that I have been supplanted, despised, censured, maligned, judged by and separated from my nearest dearest friends. By this I have found the faithfulness of Him who is the friend of friends . . . and to be content that He to whom all hearts are open . . . now sees . . . the uprightness of my intentions to all mankind.[8]

During these days Whitefield was assisted by a young man, John Cennick. Cennick was a very gracious man, but a powerful preacher, and the anointing of God was upon him. From this time onward he played a very important part in Whitefield's life.

Whitefield pressed on with his ministry, and by the time he had been in England four and a half months, his work had returned to so healthy a state that he felt able to leave it and respond to the many invitations he had received from Scotland.

The effects of Whitefield's visit to Scotland were of the happiest nature.

The dead, cold Moderatism of the predominant body in the Church was pervaded by the electric influence of a style of preaching that commanded and compelled attention; the Evangelical party was encouraged and strengthened; and the Secession itself, although he refused to shut himself up within its pale, found its best religious principles enforced by so effective and yet so disinterested an advocate.

It was the commencement of a better day in the religious history of Scotland, the blessings of which we still continue to enjoy.

Sketches of the Life and Labours of the Rev George Whitefield c. 1850

11

Scotland

*W*hitefield reached Edinburgh July 29, 1741. He still manifested certain characteristics that were not fully mature, for he was yet but twenty-six.

He had been invited to Scotland by several persons, but especially by two celebrated Presbyterian ministers, Ralph and Ebenezer Erskine. He had corresponded with them, stating in 1739, "Received an excellent letter from the Rev Ebenezer Erskine ... acquainting me of his preaching last week to fourteen thousand people. Blessed be God, there are other field preachers in the world besides myself."

The Erskines, however, were in conflict with the National Church. For some years there had been a drift in the Church which allowed a laxity in doctrine and practice, and the people who favored this condition were known as "Moderates." But they were opposed by several others who were termed "Evangelicals" — men who held to the fundamental doctrines of Christianity, believed in prayer, and lived in separation from the world. The Moderates were a majority and held the important positions in the government of the Church.

Ralph and Ebenezer Erskine were leaders of the opposition to the Moderates. They were men of deep learning, striking appearance, and unflinching convictions, and from both sides of the family the blood of nobility flowed in their veins. During the 1730s they and some eight ministers who stood with them had been suspended from the ministry because of their protests. Thereupon they set up their own ecclesiastical body, "The Secession Church." Their churches were crowded, and they carried their protest throughout much of Scotland as they contended against the officials of the Church.

The Erskines welcomed the association with Whitefield, and Ralph, in inviting him, said,

Come, if possible, dear Whitefield, come. There is no face on earth I would desire more earnestly to see. Yet ... such is the situation among us that unless you come with a design to meet and abide with us of 'The Associate Presbytery' I would dread the consequences of your coming, lest it should seem equally to countenance our persecutors. Your fame would occasion a flocking to you, to whatever side you turn. . . .[1]

In reply Whitefield stated,

This I cannot altogether agree to. I come only as an occasional preacher, to preach the simple Gospel to all who are willing to hear men of whatever denomination. It will be wrong for me to join in a reformation, as to church government. . . . I write this that there may not be any misunderstanding between us.[2]

But, as the Erskines feared, there were also others who invited Whitefield to Scotland. Several men among the Evangelicals, although they deplored the spiritual declension of the Church, were unwilling to leave it, and they likewise urged him to come.

In fact, when Whitefield reached Edinburgh, it was not the Erskines but a company of these Evangelicals who met him. We are told, "Several persons of distinction most gladly received him and would have had him preach at Edinburgh immediately."

Although Whitefield agreed to do so later, he went first to preach for Ralph Erskine at Dunfermline, and in a letter to John Cennick he stated,

As the Messrs. *Erskines* gave me the first invitation to Scotland . . . I was determined to give them the first offer of my poor ministrations. Accordingly, I went yesterday to Dunfermline, where dear Mr Ralph Erskine hath got a large meeting house. He received me very lovingly. I preached to a thronged assembly. . . . After I had done prayer and named my text, the rustling made by opening the Bibles all at once, quite surprised me: a scene I was never witness to before.[3]

Following the church service the Erskines declared they wished to talk to Whitefield at length, that they might "set him right about church government and the Solemn League and Covenant." He replied that he was to preach in Edinburgh that evening, but would return and meet the Associate Presbytery in a few days.

As he left the church he was greeted by a large company of friends, among whom were some of the nobility. He also reported,

> A portly well-looking Quaker, taking me by the hand, said, 'Friend George, I am as thou art; I am for bringing all to the life and power of the everliving God: and therefore, if thou wilt not quarrel with me about my hat, I will not quarrel with thee about thy gown.' I wish all of every denomination were thus minded.

Whitefield met with the Associate Presbytery as planned. He spoke of them as "A set of grave venerable men." They immediately began to present their doctrine of church government and the Solemn League and Covenant, but he told them they might save themselves the trouble, for he had no scruples on the subject. He asked them what they would have him do, and the answer was that he was to preach only for them till he had further light. He asked why only for them. To which Ralph Erskine replied that "they were the Lord's people." He stated that he was "determined to go out into the highways and hedges; and that if the Pope himself would lend him his pulpit," he would "gladly proclaim the righteousness of Christ therein."

He later reported,

> Soon after this the company broke up; and one of these otherwise venerable men immediately went into the meeting house and preached upon these words, 'Watchman, what of the night?' But the good man so spent himself in talking against prelacy, the common prayer book, the surplice, the rose in the hat and such like externals, that when he came to invite poor sinners to Jesus Christ his breath was so gone that he could scarce be heard. . . .
>
> The consequence of all this was an open breach. I retired, I wept, I prayed and after preaching in the fields sat down and ate with them, and then took a final leave.[4]

Following the separation from the Associate Presbytery, Whitefield entered into an active cooperation with the Evangelicals in the Church.

Certain of these men, realizing the largest churches would not be sufficient for the crowds that would throng to hear him, had already arranged for him to preach in a park, and tiers of seats had been

erected. Some fifteen thousand were present on the Sunday evening
and almost as many each evening of the week. After two weeks had
passed he wrote to Howell Harris, saying, "It would make your heart
leap for joy to be now in Edinburgh. I question if there be not
upwards of 300 in this city seeking after Jesus. Every morning I have
a levee of wounded souls."

Whitefield's activities in Scotland provide further evidence of the
carefulness with which he planned his ministry. After three weeks in
Edinburgh, using that city as his base he went out on a series of one-
week missions in different directions — northwest to Falkirk and
Stirling, north to Perth and Crieff, and then still further north to Cupar
and Dundee. The fourth week he spent in the west, in and around
Glasgow, and the fifth in "the south — in Galshiels and adjacent
towns." After another week in Edinburgh, he made a three-week circuit northeast to Aberdeen, with pauses to preach at Cupar and
Dundee and other places en route. Instead of his ministry being hap-
hazard, as certain authors have supposed, it was planned with care,
and in this instance it enabled him to reach the cities and several of
the towns of the settled portion of Scotland.

A man who accompanied Whitefield to Aberdeen gives us a side-
light on his laboring. He says:

> In several places as he came along, the Lord, I thought, countenanced
> him in a very convincing manner, particularly at a place called Lundie
> . . . where a considerable number of serious Christians, hearing he was
> to come that way, spent most part of the night before in prayer.
>
> Although his preaching there was only in a passing way, having to
> ride to Dundee after it, and it was betwixt three and four before he
> reached the place, yet he had but scarce well begun before the power
> of God was indeed very discernible. Never did I see such a pleasing
> melting in a worshipping assembly. There was nothing violent in it, or
> like what we may call screwing up the passions: for it evidently
> appeared to be deep and hearty, and to proceed from a deeper spring.[5]

Among Whitefield's hearers in Scotland there were several "per-
sons of great rank." Lord Leven, for instance, was a senator of the
College of Justice, a lord of police for Scotland, and also His
Majesty's commissioner to the General Assembly of the Church of
Scotland. Yet despite his prominence Whitefield did not fail to deal

faithfully with his soul, and from the evangelist's letters we notice the following excerpts:

> Though nature calls for rest, yet love and gratitude oblige me to sit up and answer your Lordship's letter.
>
> . . . Your Lordship is in a dangerous situation. A fear of contempt, and a love for honour, falsely so called, render religion unfashionable amongst the rich and polite part of mankind. But the blood of Jesus is almighty and makes the soul more than conqueror. . . . The blessed Spirit is now striving with you and saying, 'My son, give me thy heart; what hast thou to do any more with idols?'
>
> Take courage, then, my Lord, and fear not to follow a crucified Jesus without the camp, bearing His reproach . . . be not ashamed of Jesus or His Gospel. O that you may find it to be the power of God to your salvation.[6]

In a similar manner Whitefield dealt with other members of the Scottish aristocracy.

Of course, in Scotland, as elsewhere, Whitefield faced bitter opposition from certain classes of people. This was manifest from several members of the clergy, and John Willison, a prominent evangelical minister, wrote,

> He is hated and spoken against by all the episcopal party, and even most of our clergy [Church of Scotland] do labour to diminish him; and this is not to be wondered at, seeing his incessant labour for Christ and souls is such a strong reproof to them; besides what he says publicly against the sending out of unconverted ministers and the preaching of an unknown Christ: this must be galling to them.[7]

Moreover, there was hostility from men of the world. Since Whitefield, wherever he thought it expedient, took up an offering for the Orphan House, there were loud assertions that the money would never get to the orphans, but would go into his own pocket. But Whitefield wrote,

> Mr Willison wishes there may be a private contribution for myself, but I will not admit of any such thing. I make no purse; what I have I give away. Freely I have received, freely I desire to give. 'Poor, yet making many rich' shall be my motto still.[8]

Whitefield was in Scotland for just under three months. As he prepared to leave, the fruits of his ministry under God were widely evident. For instance, the matron of a rescue home for children — youngsters who previously had lived on the street — told him that she was "now awakened by the voice of prayer and praise." Likewise the overseer of the boys stated that "they meet together every night to sing and pray, and that when he goes to their rooms at night to see if all be safe, he generally disturbs them at their devotions."

And after he left Scotland a minister wrote to say, "Religion in this city revives and flourishes. . . . New meetings for prayer and spiritual conference are erecting everywhere. Religious conversation has banished slander and calumny from several tea-tables, and Christians are not ashamed to own their Lord. . . ."

Another minister, speaking of the young preacher himself, said, "His calmness and serenity under all he meets with, yea, his joy in tribulation, is to me so surprising that I often think the Lord sent him to this place to teach me how to preach and especially how to suffer."

John Willison, who at first had been rather critical of Whitefield, after witnessing his ministry and coming to know him personally declared,

I look upon this youth as raised up of God for special service. I see him wonderfully fitted both in body and mind, for going through with his projects, against the greatest discouragement and difficulties.

I see the man to be all of one piece. It is truly a rare thing to see one so eminent for humility in the midst of applause; for meekness and patience under reproaches and injuries; for love to enemies; for desire to glorify Christ and save souls; acquiescing to the will of God in all cases, never fretting, but still praising and giving thanks in everything.

It is rare to see in a man such a flaming fire for God in the pulpit, and yet most easy and calm when conversing with men out of it; careful not to give offence to any of them, and yet never courting the favour of any.

This worthy youth is singularly fitted to do the work of an evangelist. And seeing the Lord has stirred him up to venture his life, reputation and his all for Christ; to refuse the best benefices in his own country, and run all hazzards by sea and land . . . I truly think we ought to honour him, and to esteem him very highly in love for his work's sake.[9]

And thus, with these spiritual fires burning behind him, Whitefield left Scotland. He was riding a fine horse, given to him by Lord Leven, but he was headed not for England, but for Wales. He intended immediately to be married — married to a widow some ten years older than himself, and we shall follow him as he moved upon this strange and unusual course.

But this I say, brethren, the time is short: it remaineth that they that have wives be as though they had none.

. . . But I would have you without carefulness. He that is unmarried careth for the things that belong to the Lord, how he may please the Lord.

But he that is married careth for the things that are of the world, how he may please his wife.

The Apostle Paul
1 Corinthians 7:29, 32, 33

(The Rev. John Berridge was a confirmed bachelor who more than once revealed his antipathy to marriage and who in his penchant for witty expression often made remarks that were more distorted than factual. Mrs. Whitefield died in 1768, but some months later Berridge said, ". . . marriage might have spoiled John and George if God had not sent them a brace of ferrets." It is well-known that Mrs. John Wesley was ill-tempered, but the evidence suggests that Mrs. Whitefield in no way deserved the offense contained in Berridge's figure. The married life of the Whitefields was clearly as happy as most.)

12
Marriage

owell Harris, following his conversion in 1735, had promised himself that henceforth he would give himself wholly over to God and that no member of the opposite sex would ever have a place in his life. But by 1739 he had fallen in love with a Welsh widow, Mrs. Elizabeth James. She was an earnest Christian, and Harris developed so sacred an affection for her that in his letters he would not put her name into writing but referred to her with a +. Her affection for him, this mighty masculine man of God, was equally strong, and had he but proposed marriage her answer undoubtedly would have been an immediate and rapturous "Yes." But he was never ready to make the proposal, and he thought instead of returning to the condition he spoke of as "Having nothing between my soul and God!"

Harris saw in Whitefield a means of escaping his entanglement. Since he thought so highly of Whitefield and was so in love with Mrs. James, he felt he could perform the greatest favor to each of them by offering to step aside and suggesting that they would make ideal marriage partners for each other. Upon Whitefield's return from America, Harris had written to him of this plan, and Whitefield arranged to meet him. As they conversed, Whitefield asked if Harris really meant to give up his friendship with Mrs. James, and being assured he did, when Whitefield's ministry took him to the west of England he crossed into Wales and visited her. He wrote to her from Scotland, believing she was God's choice for him; and he rode, as we have seen, to Wales with the intention of marrying her.

Mrs. James came of a good family and had proved an earnest and active Christian. Harris had formed several Religious Societies, and these she regularly visited, dealing especially with the women members, answering their questions and urging them to continue on in Christian practice. These were days in which Harris frequently met violent opposition, and this she also confronted and did so with courage. Harris speaks of her as ". . . having no beauty, youth or riches, none but a competency." She had her own cottage in Abergavenny, where she lived with her teenaged daughter Nancy.

Her qualities, however, were chiefly of the spiritual kind. Her letters are full of Biblical quotations and abound in the intermixture of sorrow for spiritual failure and a joy that rose almost to ecstasy. There was a tenderness about her with which she often ministered to Harris and lifted him out of his despondencies.

Whitefield had arranged that when he reached Mrs. James's home Harris would meet him there. He was prepared to marry her right away.

But Mrs. James was not as ready as he. When Harris had first spoken of turning her over to Whitefield she had said,

> . . . if you were my own father you had no right of disposing me against my will. You say ye thought of parting with her ye Lord has made as your own soul was cutting till ye Lord let you see eternity &c. Pray, think what those thoughts must give me.[1]

And now as the three of them met in her home Harris reported,

> Bro. Whit . . . full of tenderness and love and simplicity, taking her as from God, (having nothing carnal of nature in him), that he feels in his heart solid, rooted and grounded love for her.
>
> She objected much, about her regards to me & that she could not help it still. & he said he would not love her the less or be jealous and was for marrying now. . . .[2]

Thus Mrs. James was confronted with making a great decision. Would she remain in the friendship of Howell Harris, the mighty man of the Welsh hills, hoping he would someday propose marriage, or would she accept the proposal of George Whitefield, the evangelist of international prominence, and marry right away?

This was the dilemma Mrs. James faced. And by the time Whitefield had been in Abergavenny four days she had made up her mind: she agreed to marry him. To him the solemn occasion required special spiritual preparation, and in a letter to Lord Leven he said, "I find a restraint upon me now so that I cannot write. God calls me to retirement, being to enter the marriage state to-morrow."[3]

But as the wedding party (which included a few friends, and Howell Harris who was to present the bride) went to the church at Llantilio, their request to have the marriage ceremony performed met a blank refusal. Whitefield and Harris were clerical outcasts to the rector. Thereupon they rode on to Usk, where they met the same response. Then on to Llanllowel, and by evening they reached Calcott, being in each place refused. But the people rallied by seeing the party ride past their farms and through their towns, and Whitefield closed the day with an open-air meeting.

On the next day, however, they came to Caerphilly, where the clergyman, the Rev. John Smith, a friend of the revival, was willing to marry them.

The ceremony took place November 14, 1741. Harris wrote,

> . . . went with Bro. Whit, + and Bro. Sims and his wife, to be married in the Chapel to the Church past 11. Great earnestness to pray for them. When it was over we retired to sing an hymn by Bro. Cennick on marriage. Then to receive the sacrament. . . . Then Bro. Whit preached with an amazing power on Matt 9:12.[4]

And thus, with the rite finally performed, Whitefield's brief and extraordinary association with Elizabeth James came to its happy fulfillment: marriage.

Whitefield entered this new state determined that it would in no way interfere with his ministry. To Gilbert Tennent he wrote,

> I married one who was a widow, of about thirty-six years of age . . . neither rich in fortune nor beautiful as to her person, but, I believe a true child of God, and would not, I think, attempt to hinder me in his work for the world.[5]

There was no honeymoon, but Whitefield stayed at his wife's cottage for a week, preaching twice a day in the area round about. Then leaving her and her daughter there, he set out on a preaching tour to Bristol, then on to Gloucester, and finally to London. After a month he returned to Abergavenny for Christmas Day, but on the following morning he was on his way to Bristol and London again. He described his manner of life, saying, "I sleep and eat but little, and am constantly employed from morning till midnight." He apparently felt he had succeeded in his determination to continue his ministry without distraction.

Three months after the wedding Elizabeth joined him in London. This meant vacating her cottage and entering the rented lodgings he had obtained in the city. Moreover, it meant meeting his congregation: they knew he had married and that his bride was a widow some ten years older than himself, one who was spoken of as "having no beauty." We may well imagine her self-consciousness as the people — especially the women — passed their opinions of her when she first entered the Tabernacle.

Certain authors have assumed that Whitefield's marriage was not a happy one. In contradiction we notice that he referred to Elizabeth in such terms as "my help meet," "my dear partner," and "my dear yoke-fellow." To a husband and wife whose marriage brought them much contentment he stated, "Happy pair! I know by sweet experience the comforts you enjoy." And Howell Harris referred to Elizabeth as "a blessing and glory to her husband," and remarked, "Is not that marriage of Thine own making!" Several similar items could also be cited, all manifesting their married happiness.

Nevertheless, the Whitefields had their sorrows. After three years had passed Elizabeth bore a son, and in the Tabernacle Whitefield made a statement that, having named him "John," he knew he would grow up to be a great preacher — "another John the Baptist." His words proved groundless.

Elizabeth and Whitefield were then living in rented lodgings in London, but since he lacked the money to maintain even this poor housing they decided that she and John had best move to her cottage in Wales. The land was then in Winter, and they traveled in a coach that was, of course, unheated, over roads that were frozen and rutted. As Whitefield had planned, upon reaching Gloucester they broke their journey by spending a few days at The Bell Inn, which was then operated by his brother. But while they were there the baby grew sick, and despite the best efforts of a physician the baby died.

Whitefield was away preaching at the time, and when he returned to Gloucester he learned the sad news. He joined his wife in her mourning, but although she urged him to stay with her, he quoted the

Psalm, "He that goeth forth and weepeth, bearing precious seed, shall doubtless come again with rejoicing," and as usual he went out to preach. He stated,

> . . . just as I was concluding my sermon the bell struck out for the funeral. At first . . . it gave nature a shake, but looking up I recovered strength. . . . Our parting with him was solemn. We kneeled down and shed many tears. . . . And then, as he died in the house in which I was born, he was taken and laid out in the church where I was baptized, first communicated and first preached. . . . I was comforted from that passage in the Book of Kings, 'Is it well with thee? . . . Is it well with the child?' And she answered 'It is well.'[6]

Elizabeth prepared to continue her journey to her cottage alone, except for a woman who accompanied her. Whitefield, however, had given much of her furniture to needy people in Abergavenny. He sought to borrow some from friends in Gloucester, and with a measure of joy he reported obtaining a secondhand set of curtains. Yet this was the man whom many charged with becoming rich through funds given for the Orphan House.

One of Whitefield's most noticeable faults had been his practice of depending on impulses, believing they were given by God. But following the manifest failure of his certainty that his boy was to become another John the Baptist, he realized the falsity of the practice. It did not again appear throughout his life.

Mrs. Whitefield accompanied her husband, as we shall see, on his next trip to America, which kept them out of England for almost four years. But before that she accompanied him on his second visit to Scotland, witnessing with him the power and glories of the revival at Cambuslang.

The sacrament at Cambuslang was an event never to be forgotten. Thirteen ministers were present on Friday, Saturday and Sunday, and on Monday, twenty-four. Mr Whitefield's sermons were attended with much power . . . several crying out and a great weeping being observable throughout his auditories.

While he was serving some of the tables he appeared to be so filled with the love of God, as to be in a kind of ecstasy, and he communicated with much of that blessed frame.

William McCulloch
1742

13

The Revival at Cambuslang

W hitefield reached Edinburgh on June 3, 1742. Seven months had passed since his last visit to Scotland, and during that time amazing things had taken place at two parishes near Glasgow: Kilsyth and Cambuslang.

For some time the work of God in these parishes had been at a low ebb. The Rev. William McCulloch of Cambuslang and the Rev. James Robe of Kilsyth had declared, "Things had become so bad with us that there were few that we, as ministers, could comfort as believers in Christ when we found them a-dying."

McCulloch and Robe possessed no outstanding abilities in the pulpit, but sensing their spiritual responsibility they began, in 1741, to perform their labors with increased earnestness. They declared with new fervor the holiness of God and the sinfulness of man, the atonement of Christ, and the need of the new birth.

Then came Whitefield's first visit to Scotland. He preached for a week at Glasgow, and after he left, among the people of Cambuslang and Kilsyth there remained a deeper recognition of the underlying truths of the Scriptures, and a new interest in prayer. This condition continued, and on February 18, 1742, McCulloch reported that at the close of the Bible lecture some fifty people who had come into a state of "considerable distress" went into his dining room, and he "exhorted them throughout the night." Before two months had passed he spoke of the awakened ones as numbering three hundred.

At the same time a similar work was taking place at Kilsyth. Robe reported that on Sunday, May 16, 1742,

An extraordinary power of the Spirit accompanied the word preached. There was a great mourning in the congregation. Many cried out, and these not only women, but some strong and stouthearted men. . . . The number of them was so great that I was obliged to convene them in the Kirk. . . .[1]

Like McCulloch, Robe saw many of these people brought to "a saving closure with Christ" and their lives transformed. Overjoyed he exulted,

O praise Him, and tell everyone to praise Him for His mercy to us and that He will stay a long time with us after this sort. O it is a precious visit: He hath wounded and will heal. O let Heaven and earth praise Him![2]

The news of these events caused several experienced ministers to visit Cambuslang and Kilsyth, seeking to discover if this was merely a burst of emotion or was truly a work of God. One who inspected this activity was Dr. John Hamilton of Glasgow, and he reported that he witnessed "a repentance that arose, not from a fear of punishment, but from a sense of dishonour done to God." Dr. John Willison stated, "I conversed with many, both men and women, young and old, and could observe nothing enthusiastic [fanatical] about them. Upon the whole I look upon the work at Cambuslang as a singular and marvelous outpouring of the Holy Spirit."

Thus Cambuslang and Kilsyth and in turn much of southern Scotland was prepared for Whitefield's further ministry. Mrs. Whitefield accompanied him. They traveled by coastal vessel, and he wrote, "On board I spent most of my time in secret prayer. . . . Pray that I may be very little in my own eyes, and not rob my dear Master of any part of his glory."

He immediately launched into his ministry, preaching twice a day in Edinburgh's Orphan House Park and expounding each evening. He also visited Glasgow, where he was welcomed "in the name of 20,000," and both there and at several towns en route he witnessed spiritual results.

Whitefield also wrote to Ebenezer Erskine. "I highly value and honour you," he said. "I applaud your zeal for God, and though in some respects I think it to be levelled against me, yet I feel no resentment, and would joyfully sit down and hear you and your brethren preach. . . . I earnestly pray for you. I could drop a tear. O when shall the time come when the watchmen will see eye to eye?"[3]

The arrival of Whitefield at Cambuslang provoked a still greater enthusiasm among the people. Services were held outdoors in a large natural amphitheater, and during the first day he preached three times. He reported,

> Such a commotion surely was never heard of, especially at eleven at night. . . . For about an hour and a half there was much weeping, so many falling into deep distress and expressing it in various ways. . . .
>
> Mr McCulloch preached after I had ended, till past one in the morning, and then could scarce persuade them to depart. All night in the fields might be heard the voice of prayer and praise. Some young ladies were found by a gentlewoman praising God at break of day. She went and joined with them.[4]

On the following Sunday the Lord's Supper was observed. It will readily be seen that the scores of persons who had recently been converted would participate with the strongest fervor in this ordinance since it spoke, as McCulloch expressed it, "of Christ as their loving and beloved Lord, reigning in them, reigning over them and reigning for them." Several ministers came also, and two platforms were set up for preaching. The people who intended to partake of the Lord's Supper were examined by pastors, and admission to the Table was by metal tokens, given only to those who gave evidence of being born again.

Services were held throughout the Saturday, the Communion, together with preaching, was conducted on Sunday, and a great final service closed the celebration on the Monday. In a letter to John Cennick Whitefield reported,

> On the Sabbath day there were undoubtedly upwards of twenty thousand people. The holy sacrament was celebrated in the fields.
>
> When I began to serve a table the people so crowded upon me that I was obliged to desist and go to preach, whilst the ministers served the rest of the tables. There was preaching all day by one or another, and in the evening, when the sacrament was over, at the request of the ministers I preached to the whole congregation.
>
> On the Monday morning I preached again, but such a universal stir I never saw before. You might have seen thousands bathed in tears . . . mourning over a pierced Saviour.[5]

Such circumstances moved McCulloch to say, first concerning the work before Whitefield's arrival at Cambuslang,

> I have reason to believe that upwards of five hundred souls have been awakened, brought under a deep conviction of sin, and a feeling sense of their lost condition. Most of these have also, I trust, been savingly brought home to God. I do not include in this number such as have been found to be mere pretenders, nor such as have had nothing in their exercise beyond a dread of hell.

And concerning the period of Whitefield's ministry he stated that he did not include them in the number, "because I cannot pretend" to compute them.

Whitefield then went on to preach in other parts of Scotland, and in a month's time he returned to Cambuslang for another Communion service. People came from various sections of the country, many of them walking immense distances, and the total attendance was estimated at thirty thousand. Worship began at 8:30 on the Sunday morning, and the last table was being served at sunset. There were three platforms erected this time, and preaching was conducted throughout the day.

One of the pastors who took part was the very elderly John Bonar — the great-great-grandfather of the now well-known Horatius and Andrew Bonar. He was very frail, and it took him three days to ride the eighteen miles from his home in Torphichen. But being "helped to get up to the platform, he preached three times and with great life."

Again the expression of strong emotions at Cambuslang caused various ministers to examine the persons who experienced them. Dr Alexander Webster reported,

> They spoke under a painful sense of sin, not only as the ruin of the creature, but as dishonouring to a kind and loving Saviour. . . . They cannot bear the thought of having so long rejected the Son of God, and despised his endearing calls as set forth in the Gospel.
>
> Being persuaded that he is the only Redeemer they breathe after him under every character; as a king upon his throne, clothed with authority to reign, as well as a priest on the cross, endowed with ability to save. . . . Sensible of their utter inability to believe, how earnestly do

they pray, 'Open the everlasting doors of our heart: Come in, thou blessed of the Lord: Be our God and our portion.'[6]

Certainly some persons suffered extreme emotions during this work at Cambuslang, some in prolonged weeping and almost losing consciousness, but James Robe pointed out that these were only one in five of the number whom they considered to have experienced conversion at this time. The experience of most was much less severe, and the reports of these events were marked by such phrases as "a good deal of decency and regularity," "the spiritual glory of this solemnity," and "profound reverence on every countenance."

Moreover, the Scriptures used in the preaching were not those that particularly speak of judgment. At this second Communion Whitefield preached from, "If I wash thee not thou hast no part with me," and Robe from, "Yet it pleased the Lord to bruise him." Old Mr. Bonar's text was, "Saw ye him whom my soul loveth?," and the other men used such texts as, "Who shall lay anything to the charge of God's elect?," "Acquaint now thyself with him, and be at peace," and "The friend of the bridegroom rejoiceth greatly because of the bridegroom's voice." Here were Scriptures that depict the glory of the believer's association with Christ, and the phrase "joy unspeakable and full of glory" occurs frequently in the Cambuslang records.

Nevertheless, even while Whitefield was thus experiencing the blessing of God he still met opposition. The men of the Associate Presbytery issued a thirty-two-page pamphlet, *The Declaration, Protestation, and Testimony of the Suffering Remnant of the anti-Popish, anti-Lutheran, anti-Prelatic, anti-Whitefieldian, anti-Erastian, anti-Sectarian, true Presbyterian Church of Christ in Scotland*. They asserted that "his foul, prelatic hands" had administered the Sacrament to Presbyterians, and that "He is but a scandalous idolater, being a member of the idolatrous Church of England. He is a limb of Anti-Christ, a boar, and a wild beast. . . ."[7] And they asserted the old canard that the money he claimed was for the orphans went largely into his own pocket.

Whitefield made no reply to these men, but in a letter to a friend he stated, "The dear Messrs. Erskine have dressed me in very black colours. Dear Men, I pity them."

Likewise seven pamphlets written in Scotland appeared, each of them caricaturing him. But two that were written in America also gained circulation in Scotland. They asserted that harmful fanatical practices had sprung up in the Colonies in the wake of Whitefield's ministry and that several young men had authorized themselves to preach and were gathering hearers and working them into a frenzy. In view of the extreme emotions experienced at Cambuslang, there were many Scotsmen ready to believe these charges.

But despite such assertions, the great spiritual value of the revival at Cambuslang was evident for all to see. It was not the fruit of sensationalism, showmanship, or entertainment. Rather, as McCulloch stated, ". . . this work was begun and carried on under the influence of the great and substantial doctrines of Christianity." These were the truths preached by McCulloch and Robe, by the various men who took part at Cambuslang, and, above all, by Whitefield.

Nine years later McCulloch again assessed the movement he had witnessed, and he wrote,

> This work embraced all classes, all ages and all moral conditions. Cursing, swearing and drunkenness were given up by those who had come under its power. It kindled remorse for acts of injustice, it won forgiveness from the vengeful. It bound pastors and people together with a stronger bond of sympathy. It raised an altar in the household. It made men students of the Word of God and brought them in thought and purpose and effort into communion with their Father in heaven.
>
> True, there was chaff among the wheat, but the watchfulness of ministers detected it, and quickly drove it away.
>
> And for long years afterwards, humble men and women who dated their conversion from the work at Cambuslang, walked among their neighbours with an unspotted Christian name, and then died peacefully in the arms of One they had learned in the revival days to call Lord and Saviour.[8]

As there are so many living stones, it may be time to think of putting them together. May the great Builder of the Church guide and direct us.

Whitefield, to Howell Harris
September 1742

I was stunned to see his amazing wisdom, wherein he is taught to manage the Church, doing all calmly and wisely, following the Lord.

Howell Harris, on Whitefield
1743

14

The First Organizing of Methodism

*U*pon returning to London, Whitefield thrust himself into the work he had been doing — not only preaching the gospel, but also forming Societies and building them into an organization.

The center of his operations was, of course, the Tabernacle at Moorfields. We read of his congregation there as amounting to two and three thousand, and of special occasions when even more flooded in. Here were buildings more crowded than public authorities would allow today.

To the Tabernacle building Whitefield had already added another structure — the Society Room. The public attended the general services, but admission to the Society was reserved for members and required being periodically updated by steady attendance and a consecrated life. The Society was divided into Bands and Classes.

The Tabernacle conducted two schools (one for boys and one for girls), maintained a Book Room, and operated an organization for the help of the poor. It also had a workshop and a small employment exchange. All these activities were managed with planning and order. Howell Harris said,

> The single men meet together in Bands, and the married too apart, and once a week they all meet together. . . . Also the Leaders of every Band meet the Minister so that he knows the state of every one. The same order is also observed among the women, and once a week the Men and Women Bands meet all together.
>
> The Poor likewise is carefully looked after, as to soul and body, by Persons laid apart to that end. The Treasurer is also to receive, and lay

out the Money, and all things so ordered that tis easie and sweet, and no Hurry too.

And here are above 100 Scholars taught, Boys and Girls, and a Room for the Master, with a Bed &c., so that tis a Heaven to live here.[1]

The *Minutes of the Tabernacle* contain a section entitled "Weekly Exercise of the Ministry." It lists nineteen tasks, either of preaching or meeting with Tabernacle officers or organizations, which the minister and his one or two assistants were to perform each week. Since several of the preaching occasions took place at Societies distant from the Tabernacle, there was also the necessity of much traveling. This schedule of activity had been planned and instituted by Whitefield, and it was operated with strict regularity.[2]

There had been in England several groups termed "Religious Societies," and since the beginning of his ministry Whitefield had urged the awakened and converted persons to attend them. By this means several old Societies were greatly enlarged and many new ones were formed.

Upon his return from his second mission to America, still further new Societies began to be formed, and, as others of the former Societies had done, they expressed their desire to be under his leadership. These were increasing noticeably in number, and he stated, "We are likely to have settled Societies in several places." Accordingly, by the end of 1742 there were many of these bodies, and the public spoke of them as "Whitefieldian Methodist Societies." Of course, Methodism was not yet a separate denomination, but considered itself a movement within the Church of England. It was known for its loyalty to the evangelical faith, the holiness of its life, and its aggressiveness in declaring the gospel. Yet, persons of other denominations — Independents, Presbyterians, Baptists, and Quakers — who held to these principles were also termed "Methodists." Moreover, by this time John Wesley had largely ceased using the title "The United Societies" and was increasingly calling his work "Methodist."

Whitefield's Societies, though formed in so short a time, were located in various parts of England. Together with the Tabernacle, four others were established in places adjacent to London, and the same circumstance was true also of Bristol and Gloucester. Moreover, the *Minutes of the Tabernacle* contain "An Account of the

Societies in Connexion together under the Care of the Reverend Mr Whitefield." This "Account" lists Societies not only in the three chief centers, but also in Devon, Cornwall, Oxfordshire, Wiltshire, Buckinghamshire, Staffordshire, and Shrewsbury — thirty-six Societies in all that were established by 1743.[3]

The "Account" also lists "Places for Preaching where Societies are not Settled" and mentions another twenty-five such locations, and these likewise were in various parts of England.

This group of more than sixty Societies and Preaching Places were ministered to by more than fifty preachers.[4]

Some fifteen or so of these men devoted their full time to their spiritual labors. Most of the others continued in their secular employment, but preached several times during each week; some of them also walked several miles each Saturday to be at their appointed places for the Lord's day. A few were associated with Harris's work in Wales as well as with Whitefield's in England. Four of these men — John Cennick, John Croom, Andrew Kinsman, and William Hogg — exercised ministries of extraordinary spiritual power, and their lives are worthy of wider study and lasting commemoration.

These men were spoken of as "Whitefield's preachers" and were referred to in each issue of *The Weekly History* as "The Exhorters and Assistants in Connection with Mr Whitefield." Here then were the first of an order of men that later became widely known as "The Methodist Circuit Riders."

Even though by 1750 Whitefield ceased giving leadership to this movement, a great many people still considered themselves his followers. An Englishman, one who was opposed to him, writing in 1756, stated,

It is generally reported that Mr Whitefield has a hundred thousand followers, most of whom, before his preaching, were the vilest of mankind, but are now sober and religious persons, good members of society and good subjects of the king. It is also said that Mr Wesley's preaching has had as good an effect on like numbers. . . .[5]

The extensiveness of Whitefield's organization is evident in the following statements. In 1743 John Syms, Whitefield's secretary, declared, "There are few or no Counties in England or Wales where there is not a work begun." Likewise, in 1744 "A Gentleman of

Pembroke College, Oxford" charged Whitefield with ". . . travelling over all counties to establish newfangled societies." And in the same year Dr. Edward Wigglesworth, president of Harvard College in America, speaking to Whitefield, declared, "You have in all parts of England and Wales, as far as your interest reached, formed your followers into bands and associations . . . and have set over them exhorters, superintendents and visitors; and are yourself *Grand Moderator* over all."

There was much truth in Wigglesworth's term "Grand Moderator over all," for Whitefield did exercise an effective leadership. But it was not a leadership of the giving of commands; rather, it was one of rich affection and a holy example. Most of the people and of the preachers in his organization had been converted under his ministry, and, holding him in such high esteem and witnessing in him an embodiment of so much of their own Christian ideal, they were happy to follow him.

The movement was divided into four Associations. Quarterly Association meetings were held alternately at London, Bristol, Wiltshire, and Gloucester. Each Association had a superintendent who had the oversight of several exhorters. Reports were sent from each Association to John Syms in London, who in turn informed Whitefield of their contents.

Whitefield's organizing abilities were wanted also by the brethren in Wales. They planned to meet in December 1741 in order to organize their work more effectively, and they urged him to be present. But being unable to do so, he wrote them a letter:

> . . . The affairs you meet about are of the utmost importance. One great matter is to know what particular office and to what particular part Jesus Christ has called each of you. . . . Different persons have different gifts and graces. Some have popular gifts fit for large auditories. Others move best in a more contracted sphere, and may be exceedingly useful in private Societies.
>
> Those who are called out to act in a public manner, I think ought to give themselves wholly to the work. Others who can only serve privately may mind their secular employ and give their leisure time to the service of the Church. . . .
>
> I wish you would meet monthly, if not all together, yet in little bodies. I am now about to settle a monthly meeting at Bristol and London

where correspondents' letters are to be read and prayer made accordingly. If you had monthly meetings, each exhorter and labourer might communicate his success, an abstract might be sent over to England, and we in turn would send you an abstract of our affairs. Unity would thereby be promoted, love increased and our hands strengthened. All this may be done without a formal separation from the established Church.[6]

Certain practices which became important elements in early Methodism — the distinction between "Public" and "Private" exhorters, the Monthly Conference, and the Letter Reading Day — are here suggested for the first time.

Although the men in Wales held their meeting, their work was not finished. They wrote to Whitefield, again stating it was imperative that he be present and asking him to appoint the date. Howell Harris stated they wanted him to come "and settle all in order," and his statement indicates the function they especially wanted him to perform. Accordingly, they met at Watford in South Wales on January 5, 1743. They were eight in number — four ordained and four laymen — and by unanimous desire Whitefield served as moderator and preached each morning and each evening.

Harmony marked the gathering, and an extensive system of rules and regulations was drawn up. The ordained ministers were to be "Overseers," each with a "district" under his control. The offices of "Superintendent" and "Exhorter" were established, men were appointed to fill them, and the territory for which each was responsible was allotted. The "Exhorters" were divided into two categories — "Public" and "Private," and the terms of admission to the office were defined. There were to be Monthly Conferences on the local level, Quarterly Conferences taking in a wider area, and an Annual Conference that included the entire movement.

Moreover, Whitefield was urged to return for a further such meeting. The same men met at Watford again in three months' time, and at this gathering the Welsh and English branches of the movement were linked together, thus bringing into being the organization known as "The Calvinistic Methodist Association." Whitefield was appointed moderator for life, and Harris was to act in this capacity in his absence.

This was an historic achievement. In the prevailing assumption that Wesley was the leader in developing Methodist organization, we do well to notice that, as the Rev. Luke Tyerman (a strongly-Wesleyan historian) states, "It is a notable fact that the first Calvinistic Methodist Association was held eighteen months before Wesley held his first Methodist Conference."

In the carelessness with which men have dealt with Whitefield it has long been assumed that he had no ability as an organizer and that he formed no Societies. But now that we look further into the evidence we find the opposite to be true. We discover that his life was governed by order and planning and that he proved to be the first organizer of Methodism.

If Methodism had not come into contact with the mob it would never have reached that section of the English people which most needed salvation. The 'Religious Societies' shut up in their rooms, would never have reformed the country.

It was necessary that a race of heroic men should arise, who would dare to confront the wildest and most brutal of men, and tell them the meaning of sin, and show them the Christ of the Cross and of the Judgement Throne.

The incessant assaults of the mob on the Methodist preachers showed they had reached the masses. With a superb courage, rarely equalled on the battlefield, the Methodist preachers went again and again to the places from which they had been driven by violence, until their persistence wore down the antagonism of their assailants. Then, out of the once furious crowd, men and women were gathered whose hearts the Lord had touched.

John S. Simon
The Revival of Religion in England in the Eighteenth Century

15

Meeting the Mob

Although the leaders of early Methodism were of differing doctrinal persuasions, in another matter they were alike: they all met physical opposition with unflinching courage.

This was true first of Howell Harris. In Wales he was attacked by ruffians, hated by clergy, and brought before magistrates. And in 1741, at the town of Bala, the local clergyman opened a barrel of beer on the main street and used it to entice the mob to attack Harris.

> The women were as fiendish as the men, for they besmeared him with mire, while their companions belaboured him with their fists and clubs, inflicting such wounds that his path could be marked in the street by the crimson stains of his blood. The enemy continued to persecute him, striking him with sticks and with staves, until overcome with exhaustion he fell to the ground. They still abused him, though prostrate. . . .[1]

In London, even while he was ministering in the Tabernacle, Harris was violently opposed. More than once the mob came beating on the Tabernacle doors during a service, forced their way in, and attacked the people with staves. Amid these dangers Harris was unmoved, and of one such occasion he reported:

> Had bullets been shot at me, I felt I would not move. Mob raged. Voice lifted up, and though by the power going with the words my head almost went to pieces, such was my zeal that I cried, 'I'll preach Christ till to pieces I fall!'[2]

Perhaps such courage was to be expected from the powerfully masculine Harris, but it was equally evident in the inoffensive John

Cennick. Cennick reported an instance in which he and Harris were preaching in the Wiltshire town of Swindon:

> The mob fired guns over our heads, holding the muzzles so near to our faces that we were made as black as tinkers with the powder. We were not affrighted, but opened our breasts, telling them we were ready to lay down our lives . . . then they played an engine on us, which they filled out of the stinking ditches. While they played on Brother Harris I preached; and when they turned the engine on me, he preached. . . . The next day they gathered about the home of Mr Lawrence who had received us, and broke all of his windows with stones, cut and wounded four of his family, and knocked down one of his daughters.[3]

And on another occasion a butcher, hearing Cennick speak of "the blood of Christ," shouted, "If he wants blood I'll give him plenty." He ran to his shop and returned with a pailful. He attempted to throw it over Cennick, but was thwarted by a bystander and in the struggle received most of the contents on himself.

Despite the violence, Cennick knew no lessening of his courage or of his joy and triumph in the Lord.

And of course many instances of the triumphant meeting of violence could be cited from the *Journals* of John and Charles Wesley. John tells us, for instance, of being attacked by a mob in the town of Walsall. He reported,

> To attempt speaking was vain, for the noise on every side was like the roaring of the sea. So they dragged me along till we came to the town where, seeing the door of a large house open, I attempted to go in; but a man catching me by the hair, pulled me back into the middle of the mob. They made no more stop till they had carried me through the main street, from one end of the town to the other.
>
> I continued speaking all this time to those within hearing, feeling no pain or weariness. At the west end of the town, seeing a door half open, I . . . would have gone in, but a gentleman in the shop would not suffer me, saying they would pull the house down to the ground. However, I stood at the door and asked, 'Are you willing to hear me speak?' Many cried out, 'No! No! Knock his brains out! Down with him! Kill him at once!'[4]

The rioters struck repeatedly at John, and had he fallen to the ground they would have seen to it that he did not rise. Yet, throughout the entire episode he remained fully calm. Numerous instances of this nature could be cited from his *Journal.*

Charles Wesley was equally courageous in the face of violence. From several instances we notice the following situation:

> I had just named my text at St Ives (Isa. 40:1) when an army of rebels broke in on us. . . . They began in a most outrageous manner, threatening to murder the people. . . . They broke the sconces, dashed the windows in pieces, tore away the shutters, benches, poor-box, and all but the stone walls. I stood silently looking on, but mine eyes were unto the Lord. . . . They beat and dragged the women about, particularly one of great age, and trampled on them without mercy. The longer they stayed the more they raged. . . . The ruffians fell to quarrelling among themselves, broke the Town-Clerk's (their Captain's) head, and drove one another out of the room.[5]

Whitefield also experienced this kind of treatment. He tells of a mob "one hundred strong" that invaded the house his people had built at the town of Hampton. They attacked the pastor, Thomas Adams, forced him out of the building, threw him into a pond, and severely injured him. Adams wrote to Whitefield informing him of the assault.

The mob had declared that if Whitefield appeared at Hampton they would make him the prime object of their attack. But he nevertheless hurried to Adams's side. He wrote,

> No sooner had I entered the town than I heard the blowing of horns and the ringing of bells for the gathering of the mob. . . . I preached on a large grass platform. 'And seeing the grace of God, he exhorted them with full purpose of heart to cleave unto the Lord.'
>
> I finished my sermon and pronounced the blessing just as the ringleader of the mob broke in upon us. . . .
>
> I went into the house and preached upon the stair case to a large number of serious souls; but these real troublers of Israel soon came in to mock and mob us. But . . . power being given us from above, I leapt down stairs, and all fled away before me. However, they continued making a noise about the house till midnight, abusing the poor people as they went home, and broke one young lady's arm in two places.

Brother Adams they threw a second time into the pool; he received a deep wound in his leg. John C[room]'s life, that second Bunyan, was much threatened. Young W— H— they wheeled in a barrow to the pool side, lamed his brother and grievously hurt several others.

Hearing that two or three clergymen were in town, one of whom was a Justice of the Peace, I went to them. But instead of redressing, they laid the cause of all the grievances at my door. But by the help of God I shall still persist in preaching myself and in encouraging those who I believe are truly moved by the Holy Ghost.[6]

Whitefield's entire evangelistic life was an evidence of his physical courage. He met this kind of treatment on numerous occasions in both Wales and England, and we shall later see him meeting it also in Ireland.

Our hearts go out, however, to the poor Methodist people and their children who almost daily suffered the violence of evil opposers. Whitefield had a growing work at Exeter, and a man who was not one of its members wrote a report of an attack upon its people. He stated,

The rioters violently entered the Methodist meeting-house, interrupted the minister with obscene language, and fell upon him in a most furious manner with blows and kicks. They treated every man they could lay their hands upon with such abuse and indignity as is not to be expressed.

But what is more than all was their abominable treatment of the poor women. Some were stripped quite naked. Others, notwithstanding their most piercing cries for mercy were forcibly held by some of the wicked ruffians, while others turned their petticoats over their heads and forced them to remain in that condition . . . the poor creatures being afterward dragged through the [sewer]. . . . Towards the close of the evening one of the mob forced a woman up into the gallery, and attempted other outrages, three different times. After many struggles, she freed herself, leaped over the gallery and so made her escape. . . .

The riot continued for several hours. The mob had their full swing. It is true no one was actually murdered, but the whole Society were put into great danger and fear of their lives.[7]

Moreover, this kind of treatment was experienced in all branches of the revival. Harris's people, Whitefield's people, Wesley's people, and the Moravians all suffered at the hands of the mob, and in 1743 Whitefield decided the time had come to take the rioters to court.

First, he called his preachers to gather in London for a time of consultation and prayer. He also sent out a request to all his Societies, urging the people to be much in prayer about the matter. Then he launched charges against the men who had been active in the riot against Thomas Adams and his Society.

The defense, using two lawyers and several witnesses, argued: (1) that the Methodists were known everywhere to be fanatics; (2) that the accused had acted for the welfare of the community in opposing them; (3) that the Methodists began the tumult by attacking the accused, who in turn merely defended themselves.

The prosecution called five witnesses, three of whom were not Methodists. The outcome of the trial was that the jury brought in all defendants guilty of the whole information lodged against them. It was a complete victory for the Methodists.

Whitefield then had the right to prefer damages against the rioters. But having shown these men that they were subject to England's courts of law, he chose to forgive them and let the matter drop.

This victory was strategic in the life of early Methodism. Had the rioting continued unchecked, the work would have suffered. But now the perpetrators knew they were not able, as they had assumed, to escape all punishment, and although the violence did not cease, from this point onward it was increasingly curtailed.

In the opening months of 1744, however, Whitefield recognized that he must soon return to America. He was being blamed — though falsely — for fanaticism that had broken out in the Awakening, and he had no choice but to deal with it personally.

But as he prepared to leave, he faced the question of whom he should appoint to lead the work in his absence. He thought, of course, of Howell Harris, but Harris was busy with his own work in Wales. Whitefield's next choice was John Cennick. Cennick possessed outstanding abilities as a preacher and was invariably gracious in his dealings with other men. But Whitefield had reason to ask himself if Cennick could handle the questions that might arise among the exhorters and if he could exercise a strong enough leadership of the large movement. Whitefield had doubts on these matters, but Cennick was the best man available, and therefore the evangelist asked him to accept the care of the Tabernacle and the oversight of Whitefieldian Methodism until he himself should return.

Whitefield was to sail from Plymouth, and his wife was to accompany him on this trip to America. But upon reaching the port, since war had broken out with France they were informed the vessel would not sail till a naval convoy arrived. As matters turned out, they were left waiting for six weeks.

The six weeks began with a brutal attack in which Whitefield was nearly murdered. An officer from a man-of-war came at night to his place of lodging, seeking an interview. Whitefield had retired, but he had the landlady show the man up to his room. They began to converse, but, Whitefield reports,

> He suddenly rose up, uttering the most abusive language, calling me *dog, rogue, villain*, &c, and beat me most unmercifully with his gold-headed cane. But my hostess and her daughter hearing me cry *murder*, rushed into the room and seized him by the collar; however, he disengaged himself from them, and repeated his blows upon me.[8]

A second attacker also appeared, but before the two men could injure Whitefield any further, the noise of the assault aroused people in the homes round about, and their presence frightened the assailants away. These men undoubtedly intended to murder Whitefield. Certain authors who reveal little knowledge of his life accuse him of cowardice on account of this affair, stating he had to be rescued by two women. They fail to realize that Whitefield reported the assault in a letter to an elderly Christian woman with whom he corresponded, to whom it would be natural for him to praise the landlady and her daughter and to demean himself. The constant courage that governed his ministry speaks for itself.

While he was waiting for the vessel to sail, Whitefield preached three times daily. "I preached to many thousands," he said in a letter. "A calling, inviting, persuasive gift was vouchsafed me. . . . I am continually engaged in preaching, and in talking privately with many, very many, awakened souls." Although he had never before been in Plymouth, when the six weeks were ended he left behind him a strong Society that had sprung from his labors, and another also at "the Dock" two miles distant. To this end, he had employed his time of waiting for the convoy to arrive.

Accordingly, by August 7 the vessels were ready, and Whitefield and Elizabeth embarked. She was now to experience her first overseas journey, and he was to enter a difficult situation and to endeavor to heal the wounds that had developed in the Great Awakening in America.

Whitefield's journey through New England was a tour of pacification. While preaching the same doctrines with the same emotional power, he explicitly warned his hearers from all the extremes which had been revived by the general awakening of religious interest.

. . . time and excessive labours had not dulled his enthusiasm or deprived his words and gestures of their subtle charm, but friends and enemies remarked that the asperity which formerly marred the pulpit utterances of the young reformer now gave place to a noble charity.

C. H. Maxson
Whitefield the Pacificator
1920

16

Healing the Wounds and Completing the Work in America

*A*fter a dangerous and storm-filled crossing of the Atlantic, Whitefield landed at York, New Hampshire. The date was October 26, 1744, and he was twenty-nine years old.

Nearly four years had elapsed since he had last been in America, and during that time important changes had taken place in the Great Awakening. When he had left America, a glorious spiritual work was being carried on, and it continued after his leaving. Gilbert Tennent had labored in Boston, and Thomas Prince of the Old South Church stated, "Within three months were three score joined to our communicants, the greater part of whom gave a more exact account of the work of the Spirit of God on their souls." Prince went on to describe the continuing alteration in the city and remarked,

> And thus successfully did this divine work go on in town without any lisp of a separation, either in this town or province, for above a year and a half after Mr. Whitefield left us.[1]

Likewise Jonathan Parsons of Lyme, Connecticut declared,

> I believe the people advanced more in their acquaintance with the Scriptures, and a true doctrinal understanding of the operations of the Holy Spirit in conviction, regeneration and sanctification, in six months' time than they had done in the whole of my ministry before, which was nine years.[2]

Several ministers spoke in a similar manner, telling of the spiritual work done in their own hearts, in their churches, and in their communities. Recognizing a manifest demand, the Rev. Thomas Prince began to publish a weekly paper, *The Christian History*, which largely reported these testimonies. It is evident that, as stated, the movement continued in power "for above a year and a half after Mr. Whitefield left America."

Nevertheless, other elements also entered. For example, the practice of creating noise and confusion in church services was developed. This arose from the fact that the Spirit of God had wrought an overwhelming conviction in many hearts, causing sinners to cry out. But certain persons, feeling these extreme experiences were a necessary element of revival, sought to imitate them, shouting and falling to the floor in the midst of the services.

Moreover, danger arose from the activities of a number of young men who were known as "exhorters." Most of them were basically earnest, but in general they lacked education, and some were coarse in their manners. They went forth without any authorization, and several made the denunciation of various pastors their chief function. Although the labors of some were beneficial, the activities of the exhorters, so largely undisciplined and ungoverned, were on the whole utterly detrimental to the work.

The confusion in many services and the activities of the exhorters began to bring the Awakening into disrepute. The chief difficulty arose, however, from the practices of a Rev. James Davenport.

Davenport had suffered a breakdown that affected both mind and body. But he entered the ministry and manifested such fervor that pastors and people in general knew him as "a most heavenly minded man." With the coming of the Awakening, he entered into its labors with great zeal; but it soon became evident that in his condition he could not cope with the new excitement.

Davenport's weakness was apparent first in his profession of being guided by direct revelations. He thought of himself as a great reformer and a special favorite of God, and he declared that God spoke to him in dreams and visions. His preaching frequently produced convulsions and faintings, and these phenomena he regarded as the working of the divine power. He had long suffered a fever, and his condition was aggravated by his spending whole nights in prayer and on one occasion by preaching for twenty-one hours. As he traveled, he called on ministers, demanding an account of their religious experience and publicly denouncing as unconverted all who failed to measure up to his requirements. He urged his followers to sustain the work, even if it meant defying the laws of the Colony. He was at one point arrested, and the militia was called out to protect those who examined him. In an attempt to "cure the people of their love of worldly things," he had them bring their "wigs, cloaks, breeches, hoods, gowns, rings and jewels," and these items, together with a number of evangelical books, he consumed in the fire.

Although Davenport later apologized for his foolish actions, the harm he had done was not easily removed. He had developed a considerable number of followers, and many of them likewise claimed that God spoke to them directly and that they needed no further authority for their behavior. Some were *for*, but more were *against* Davenport, and divisions took place in homes, in churches, and in the community, and the Congregationalists, the Presbyterians, and the Baptists were each divided into two opposing factions.

Whitefield, however, was being blamed for the extreme actions and for the divisions, and his accusers were not without grounds for their claims. During his previous visit Whitefield had spoken of impressions made on his mind, and this was used as a basis for the assertions of direct revelation. He had urged every Christian to be busy making the gospel known and had influenced the ministers to preach every day of the week, and this the exhorters declared was the authorization for their activity. He had rejoiced to see sinners brought into deep conviction and had denounced the presence of unconverted men in the ministry, and this, his opposers claimed, had given rise to the confusion and the separations.

Regarding these charges Whitefield stated, ". . . many good souls, both among the clergy and the laity, for a while mistaking fancy for faith and imagination for revelation, were guilty of great imprudence. Now all is laid to me as being the *primum mobile*, though there was not so much as the appearance of anything of this nature when I left New England last."

This, then, was the situation that Whitefield set about to correct. Although very unwell, he immediately accepted many invitations to preach. Soon, however, he was confined to bed. Yet here he said, "God dealt so bountifully with me that I felt a divine life distinct from my animal life, which made me, as it were, to laugh at pain. . . ." He rose from his bed, went and preached, and came home, seemingly a dying man. He lay in a semiconscious state, and a black woman came and, looking him earnestly in the face, stated, "Master, you just go to Heaven's gate. But Jesus said, 'Get you down, you must not come here yet, but go first and call some more poor Negroes!'" He gradually recovered, but he remained physically weak as he began the important work before him.

When he reached Boston, Whitefield discovered that the rumors that he was to blame for the fanaticism had caused questionings in the minds of several former supporters. Four prominent ministers — Dr. Sewall, Dr. Colman, Thomas Foxcroft, and Thomas Prince — called on him, and he reported,

> I found by what they said, that the work of God had gone on in the most glorious manner for near two years after my departure. . . .
>
> They were apprehensive that I would promote separations and that some had been encouraged to separate by my saying that I found the generality of preachers preached an unknown Christ, that Colleges had darkness in them, and that, speaking of the danger of an unconverted ministry, I said, How can a dead man beget a living child?
>
> I said I was sorry if anything I had said had been a means of promoting separations, for I was of no separating principles, but came to New England to preach the Gospel of peace and promote charity among all.
>
> We talked freely and friendly about several things, by which the jealousies they had entertained seemed in a great measure ended, and Dr Colman asked me to preach in his Meeting House.[3]

After this discussion and after hearing him preach, the confidence of these Boston pastors was restored. They realized that during his previous visit Whitefield had been a youth of merely twenty-four, and they saw that he was now more mature and possessed a wisdom which they believed would guard him from excessive expressions.

Thus accepted, Whitefield entered into a ministry in New England as extensive as that of his former days. He preached in Boston in church after church, and everywhere the buildings were crowded. In response to public demand, he began to hold a service at 6 in the morning and another at 7, and he spoke of his delight in "seeing those who had been used to lie in bed till 8 or 9, running to hear the Word in a cold winter season at break of day."

As Whitefield performed this ministry, the populace gradually realized he had no desire to perpetuate the Davenport practices, and prejudice noticeably melted away. "My conduct and my preaching," he declared, "breathed nothing but love."

Whitefield's return to Boston drew forth a host of pamphlets against him. One of these, however, was from a most prestigious source: *A Testimony from the President and Professors, Tutor, and Hebrew Instructor of Harvard College against the Reverend George Whitefield.* The *Testimony* asserted that Whitefield was "an enthusiast, a censorious, uncharitable person, and a deluder of the people," and in proof of these charges the authors stated that he depended on dreams and impressions, and they cited his assertions of "spiritual darkness" in Harvard and Yale. They also claimed he had deluded the public by his incomplete financial statements concerning his Orphan House.

Despite his continuing sickness, Whitefield wrote a reply to the *Testimony*. In this he admitted that certain elements in his earlier actions were immature and apologized for them. But he also quoted from a sermon preached by Dr. Edward Holyoke, Harvard's president, which contained statements of the existence of the same errors as the statements for which the *Testimony* accused him. His manner was not a compromising one; he stood his ground, yet his style was quiet and peace-making. Remarkably, the men who wrote the *Testimony* did not realize that they themselves were "censorious and uncharitable" in their attitude towards Whitefield.

The fact that "Harvard published against him" has been repeated times without number, but the document that Harvard later produced thanking him for his benefactions to the College has been little-known.

Moreover, while he was at Boston the people clamored for him to remain, and as an incentive they offered to build for his use the largest church anywhere in America at that time.

Whitefield remained in New England for nine months, and during that period he lived down the charge that he intended to promote fanatical practices. He set an example of a ministry which, though still characterized by constant zeal, was also governed by prudent restraint.

Upon leaving New England, Whitefield set out on a journey that was to take him, preaching as he traveled, to the Orphan House in Georgia. At New York, despite statements both for and against him in the newspapers, his congregations were as large as ever. At

Philadelphia, the people declared their desire to pay him an annual salary of £800 if he would preach to them merely six months of the year. But this offer, like that in Boston, he graciously refused.

In Virginia, Whitefield received striking evidence of the effectiveness of his printed sermons. Samuel Morris, a bricklayer, had begun the practice of reading Whitefield's sermons to people who gathered in his house. The house was soon crowded, and a new building for this purpose was built. This too became crowded, and a second, a third, and a fourth such "Reading House" was constructed, and all were immediately filled. As a result of hearing these sermons, several were moved to severe weeping, and many were soundly converted. Whitefield visited Morris and his people and remained with them five days. This was the beginning of the Presbyterian body in Virginia. Any attempt to estimate the value of Whitefield's printed sermons must take into account Samuel Morris and his Reading Houses.

Upon reaching Bethesda, Whitefield found that during his absence notable progress had been made. The buildings and grounds were a delight to behold; only a few details of construction remained to be completed, and both the Orphan House and the plantation were in excellent order.

But since arriving in America, because of the opposition Whitefield had received no offerings, and the financial need had now become acute. Accordingly he enlisted the aid of several men in England and America — some were ministers and others business-men — who agreed to contribute regularly to Bethesda.

Benjamin Franklin, however, sympathizing with Whitefield in the burden that he carried, wrote an appeal that he intended to insert in his own paper and also in other papers on both continents. But this offer Whitefield refused, feeling that advertising the institution's need seemed like suggesting that God had failed it. Thereupon Franklin made a personal gift, the sum of £75.[4]

Whitefield did, however, send copies of Franklin's appeal to several friends to be used in a private way. But that plan proved to be of little value, since it depended on the mail. England was then at war, and trans-Atlantic letters were often lost. And even mail from America to so distant a point as Savannah was notably unreliable. Likewise Thomas Noble, who had declared his desire to help and had already lent Whitefield money for Bethesda, passed away, leaving his entire estate to the Moravians. The executor of the will wrote wanting repayment of the loan within six months, and a weary Whitefield replied, "I am afraid it will be out of my power, but as we are Brethren of the same Lord and as the debt was contracted for Him I hope you will be patient with me."

In the midst of these circumstances, Whitefield was informed of a distressing circumstance in England: John Cennick had left him and his work.

Cennick, whom he had made pastor of the Tabernacle and the overseer of Whitefieldian Methodism throughout England, had not been able to handle the immense task. He possessed unusual ability as a preacher and was characterized by a holy life, undaunted courage, and unflagging zeal; but the many responsibilities proved too heavy for him. He felt the need of strong company and knew not when Whitefield would return, and since he had long found happy fellowship with the Moravian Brethren, he finally entered their movement.

Cennick wrote to Whitefield, informing him of his change of allegiance. Whitefield, whose cause suffered grievously from the loss, was disappointed, but he replied,

> Dear John:
>
> Though I am quite sick and weak in body, yet the love I owe thee for Jesu's sake constrains me to answer your last kind letter. . . .
>
> It has been thy meat and drink to preach among poor sinners the unsearchable riches of Christ. May'st thou continue in this plan, and whether I see thee or not . . . I shall always pray that the work of God shall prosper in thy hands. . . . Go where thou wilt, though thou shouldst be in the purest society under heaven, thou wilt find that the best of men are men at best. . . .[5]

Because of the loss of John Cennick, Whitefield was repeatedly urged by the officials of the Tabernacle and by Howell Harris to set sail for England. But in view of the spiritual need in America, he determined he could not yet leave.

Bethesda's financial need, however, was burdening him. Accordingly, certain friends put into action a plan which they were sure would help. "God has put it into the hearts of my South Carolina friends," he said, "to contribute liberally towards purchasing a plantation and slaves in this province, which I propose to devote to the support of Bethesda. . . . I have called it Providence."

Thus Whitefield became an owner of slaves!

Although we utterly deplore the practice, we must at least attempt to understand it as Whitefield viewed it. Until that time, virtually only the voices of a few leading Quakers had declared against slavery. The empires of history had been built upon it, and it was still practiced in virtually every country on earth. Christians in general favored it, and in the home of almost every minister in America the bulk of the manual labor was done by a slave. For some few years after his conversion, John Newton was captain of a vessel that brought slaves from Africa to their bondage in America.

The blacks at Providence, we may be sure, were treated with kindness, and many a black from neighboring plantations would undoubtedly have shouted for joy had he been informed he was being transferred there. Nevertheless, we must face the grim fact that Whitefield did not oppose slavery. He agreed with the conditions of his times, and this mark is the one dark blot upon an otherwise unspotted career.

Whitefield continued his incessant ministry, especially in the Southern and Middle Colonies. Despite constant weariness, he found the deepest joy of his life in preaching the gospel, and in the face of appeals by friends that he slacken his pace, he drove on. Here are some excerpts from his letters at that time:

I have been ranging the woods in the service of the best of Masters, who makes his work more pleasant to me every day. Everywhere almost, the door is opened for preaching. Great numbers flock to hear, and the power of an ascended Saviour attends the Word.

It is surprising how the Lord causes prejudices to subside and makes my formerly most bitter enemies to be at peace with me.

My preaching is blessed to poor souls. Amazing love! Maryland is yielding converts to the blessed Jesus.

A large living was offered me . . . if I would accept of it. But I have no thoughts of settling till I settle in glory.

The heat is trying to me. But the Lord Jesus . . . enables me to ride many miles and preach twice a day.

O that I could do more for Him! O that I was a flame of pure and holy fire, & had a thousand lives to spend in the dear Redeemer's Service. . . . The sight of so many perishing souls affects me much, & makes me long to go if possible from pole to pole, to proclaim redeeming love.[6]

Whitefield was warned, however, by his doctor, Dr. Edward Shippen, America's foremost physician (an earnest Christian and a personal friend), that he must allow himself a period of rest. So although he had stated, "I intend going on till I drop," after being unable to rise from his bed for some days he agreed to a time of change. Josiah Smith suggested he could relax best in Bermuda, and thus he agreed to spend a short time in that isle. Since Mrs. Whitefield did not particularly enjoy ocean travel, she chose to remain in Philadelphia. He intended to return for her so they could sail to England together.

Throughout these days in America, Whitefield had walked a difficult pathway. His ministry had combined fervor with prudence, and though laboring to remove unnecessary strife he had made not the least compromise of his doctrinal convictions. He had exercised zeal with wisdom, and under his example the fanaticism that had previously marred the Awakening was largely dispersed.

Early in March 1748, exhausted and unwell, Whitefield embarked for Bermuda. Thousands in America undoubtedly shared the feelings of Benjamin Franklin, who declared,

Mr Whitefield was never so generally well esteemed by persons of all ranks among us; nor did he ever leave with so many ardent wishes for his happy journey and a safe return to this place.

It is impossible to conceive what would have been the result if Whitefield and Harris had continued active chiefs of the Calvinistic Methodists. . . .

The plain facts are these: within two months after his return from America in 1748, Whitefield determined to put an end to his official relationship to Calvinistic Methodists: this determination was gradually carried out; and during the last twenty years of his life he occupied a new position.

Rev. Luke Tyerman
The Life of George Whitefield
1877

17

"Let the Name of Whitefield Perish"

*U*pon reaching Bermuda, Whitefield received a vigorous welcome and was immediately asked to preach. Accordingly he did so twice, and after dining with the governor he preached before the council and an assemblage of the island's dignitaries.

Thereafter he kept on preaching — twice and often three times a day in churches, in meeting-houses, in homes, and in the open air. He ministered in the towns and also in the unsettled areas, and again he witnessed the presence and power of God.

Even while in Bermuda, he received letters that asserted that he must return immediately to England. Whitefieldian Methodism had suffered severely through the loss of John Cennick, and recently a brilliant young preacher, William Cudmore, had also left, taking three hundred people from the Tabernacle and establishing his own Society near by. Howell Harris had given leadership to Whitefield's cause, but his time was limited, and he and the Tabernacle officials wrote declaring that Whitefield must sail for England by the first vessel available.

To do so meant that Mrs. Whitefield would be left to return home alone. But she had agreed that she would never stand in the way of her husband's work, so he embarked for England, leaving her in America.

He had come to Bermuda with the thought of keeping his doctor's orders that he rest, but throughout his two months on the island he had preached continually. And he anticipated declaring the gospel during his passage home, for he prayed, "Oh may God give me all the souls that sail with me!"

Whitefield had been out of England for four years. His people had been yearning for him to return, and when he reached London he was welcomed by crowds. Their joy rose especially from seeing that he was alive, for the news of his long illness in America had been followed by the report that he had died. *The Gentleman's Magazine*, for instance, had recently included in its "LIST OF DEATHS" "The Reverend Mr George Whitefield, the famous itinerant and Founder of the Methodists." Other papers had published similar statements.

The work of the Tabernacle immediately sprang into new life. Excited yet worshipful congregations crowded its services, and vast hosts gathered in Moorfields for Whitefield's open-air preaching. He visited Gloucester and Bristol, and in each place he found the same enthusiasm.

At the same time, Whitefield was now forced to give strong consideration as to what course he should follow. For one thing, he knew that much of the balance of his life would be devoted to America and that he could give but a portion of his time to Britain.

Moreover, Whitefield was determined not to enter a scene of conflict again. During his preceding years in England — 1741 to 1744 — although he had brought Wesley into an attitude of reconciliation, he had also sensed a constant spirit of rivalry. The same spirit had been manifest between many of the people of the Foundery and the Tabernacle, and it was evident that several of his people were waiting for his ministry to flourish again and that they intended to use it to claim a triumph over Wesley and his followers.

But Whitefield utterly deplored this whole spirit of competition between the people of God, and he resolved to overcome it.

He first felt that much difficulty would be avoided if Arminian Methodism and Calvinistic Methodism could be united. He broached the idea to Howell Harris, but received no encouragement. "It will never do," said Harris, "because neither of the sides can submit to the other head — Mr Wesley or Mr Whitefield."[1]

Since John Wesley was not in London at the time, Whitefield conferred with his brother Charles. Charles had by now matured considerably and had altered in his theological views to such an extent that some lay preachers had reported to John that he agreed with Whitefield, both as to predestination and in his opposition to the perfection teaching. This was an exaggeration, though Charles had mellowed on each of these teachings and had come to a position much nearer to that of Whitefield. As Charles and Whitefield met, their fellowship was warm and sweet, and Charles declared his willingness to enter into closer cooperation.

Whitefield also wrote to John Wesley. His letter reads, in part,

> Rev and Dear Sir:
>   My not meeting you in London was a disappointment to me. . . .
>   What have you thought about an union? I am afraid an external one is impracticable. I find by your sermons that we differ in principles more than I thought. . . .
>   My attachment to America will not permit me to abide very long in England. . . . I hope you don't forget to pray for me. You are always remembered by, Reverend and dear Sir,
>   Yours most affectionately in Christ Jesus,
>   G.W.[2]

Whitefield and Harris next arranged a conference to consider the matter. Present were John and Charles Wesley, Whitefield and Harris. Harris said of the event,

> . . . we opened our hearts about the points in dispute and saw a possibility of coming to terms . . . keeping off the controversial way, to adopt each other's expressions as much as possible, each to give up all we can. Agreed to draw up such rules as may prevent the law of love from being broken any more.
>   I mentioned my fears lest he (J.W.) should affect to be head and to be a party. Mr Whitefield mentioned his objection to his monopolising the name of Methodist to himself only.

Whitefield recognized, however, that notwithstanding this increased measure of cooperation there was little possibility of uniting the two branches of Methodism. There were deep hostilities among the people, and he also knew, as Howell Harris and Lady Huntingdon stated, that John Wesley, possessing as he did unusual gifts of administration, would not be satisfied without being first.

Accordingly, Whitefield came to a tremendous, self-sacrificing decision. He determined that he would give over his position as the head of Calvinistic Methodism, and although he would retain warm fellowship with his Societies he would no longer lead them as a

154 / George Whitefield

movement. Furthermore, he would locate some man who would serve as pastor of the Tabernacle, and its affairs would be governed by its chief men.

By this act he would free himself to preach the gospel without the least ties or organizational responsibilities, and he would become, as he said, ". . . simply the servant of all." And by this act he would spare the movement from strife and would allow John Wesley to be the one head of Methodism.

Whitefield then asked Howell Harris to take the pastorate of the Tabernacle. But Harris refused. Whitefield next offered it to three men jointly, but this invitation also was not accepted. It was evident the people of the Tabernacle would accept as their pastor no one but himself, and therefore he agreed to retain it. But he made no attempt to obtain someone to serve as president of the Calvinistic Methodist Association, and although the Societies continued, the organization began to die away.

Whitefield's renunciation of his position was strongly objected to by his people. They had borne with his four years of absence in America, and now that he was home they wanted to see him go on in his ministry and even to add new triumphs. But with his announcement their hopes were shattered. Several of them asserted that thereby he would lose his fame and that it would cause him finally to be forgotten by future generations. But he made such replies as,

Let the name of Whitefield perish, but Christ be glorified.

Let my name die everywhere, let even my friends forget me, if by that means the cause of the blessed Jesus may be promoted.

But what is Calvin, or what is Luther? Let us look above names and parties; let Jesus be our all in all — So that He is preached. . . . I care not who is uppermost. I know my place . . . even to be the servant of all.

I am content to wait till the judgement day for the clearing up of my reputation; and after I am dead I desire no other epitaph than this, 'Here lies G.W. What sort of man he was the great day will discover.'[3]

Whitefield's magnificent surrendering of his position has remained virtually unnoticed by his biographers. One, however, the Rev. Luke

Tyerman, Methodism's chief historian, has alluded to it. Yet it may well be asked, "Where in all church history do we find such magnanimous selflessness?" So noble an action is all but unknown.

By his act Whitefield saved the revival from further discord and strife. And because of it, John Wesley, not George Whitefield, is known today as "the leader and founder of Methodism."

Whitefield, however, started out afresh to fulfill his particular mission as "the servant of all."

Whitefield lived in an age of peculiar politeness, and in no one point was found wanting, so that nobles and courtiers who had studied its graces from the cradle, found themselves in these points equalled, if not eclipsed, by the natural elegance of the lowly evangelist of Methodism.

An Anonymous Scottish Author
c. 1850
Sketches of the Life and Labours of George Whitefield

18

The Gospel to the Aristocracy in England

*T*he aristocracy of eighteenth-century England were not a people likely to be attracted by the gospel. The lives of most were characterized by godlessness; yet all made much of their practice of the politeness of high society and the maintenance of their professed superiority over mere commoners. They possessed, in general, vast inherited wealth and titles, but drunkenness, gambling, and immorality were their frequent activities,

Of course, as in any class, certain of these titled elite were different. Outstanding in this regard was the Countess of Huntingdon. Since her earliest days Lady Huntingdon had remained aloof from the coarser pleasures of her peers, and she had trusted that her self-righteousness would obtain her salvation. But this assurance left her when she lay on a sickbed. In a great sense of her need she then called upon God, crying, "Lord! I believe! Help thou mine unbelief!" She cast herself upon Jesus Christ and was brought into the full assurance of salvation.

Lord and Lady Huntingdon had attended Whitefield's ministry since its beginning. But Lord Huntingdon shortly passed away, and following his death Lady Huntingdon came into a new and deep devotion to the things of God. She became a true student of the Scriptures and a woman of believing prayer.

Although Whitefield had given over the leadership of Calvinistic Methodism, another door now opened to him. Lady Huntingdon first indicated her acceptance of his ministry and her agreement with his doctrinal position by appointing him one of her chaplains. Secondly, she asked him to preach to a company of the aristocracy whom she invited to her home. Despite the tremendous weight of the task, he complied, and such was his ministry that several of his hearers expressed the desire that the occasion be repeated. In response Lady Huntingdon arranged for him to preach to them twice a week, and her drawing room constantly overflowed with these richly bejeweled, highly perfumed, and elegantly dressed members of the nobility.

These hearers may mean little to the readers of today, but we notice them and certain of their attainments in order that we may recognize something of the burden Whitefield faced in this ministry. A partial listing is as follows:

Lady Fanny Shirley, who had long been one of the reigning beauties of the Court of George the First; the Duchess of Argyle; Lady Betty Campbell; Lady Ferrers; Lady Sophia Thomas; the Duchess of Montagu, daughter of the great Duke of Marlborough; Lady Cardigan; Lady Lincoln; Mrs Boscawen; Mrs Pitt; Miss Rich; Lady Fitzwalter; Lady Caroline Petersham; the Duchess of Queensbury, daughter of the Earl of Clarendon, celebrated for her extraordinary beauty, wit, and sprightliness by Pope, Swift and Prior; the Duchess of Manchester; Lady Thanet, daughter of the Marquis of Halifax; Lady St. John; Lady Luxborough, the friend and correspondent of Shenstone, the poet; Lady Monson; Lady Rockingham, the wife of the great statesman, a woman of immense wit and pleasant temper; Lady Betty Germain, through her husband Sir John Germain the possessor of enormous wealth; Lady Eleanor Bertie, the Dowager-Duchess of Ancaster; the Dowager-Lady Hyndford; the Duchess of Somerset; the Countess Delitz, sister of Lady Chesterfield; Lady Hinchinbroke, granddaughter of the Duke of Montagu; and Lady Schaubs.

Besides these 'honourable women' there were also a similar number of men: the Earl of Bubington, famed for his architectural expenditure; George Bubb Doddington, afterwards Lord Melcombe, a friend and favourite of the Prince of Wales, and whose costly mansion was often crowded with literary men; George Augustus Selwyn, an eccentric wit, to whom nearly all the bon-mots of the day were attributed; the Earl of Holderness; Lord (afterwards Marquis) Townshend, named George after his godfather, George the First, a distinguished general in the army, a member of Parliament and ultimately Field Marshall; Charles Townshend, whom Burke described as 'the delight and ornament of the House of Commons, and the charm of every private society he honoured with his presence'; Lord St. John, half-brother to Lord

Bolingbroke; the Earl of Aberdeen; the Earl of Lauderdale; the Earl of Hyndford, Envoy Extraordinary to the King of Prussia; the Marquis of Tweedsdale, Secretary of State for Scotland; Lord Lyttleton, Secretary of Frederick, the Prince of Wales; William Pitt, the distinguished First Earl of Chatham; Lord North, First Lord of the treasury; Evelyn, Duke of Kingston; Viscount Tretham; the Earl of March; the Earl of Haddington; the Earl of Beaulieu; Baron Hume; the Earl of Sandwich, subsequently Ambassador to the Court of Spain, First Lord of the Admiralty and Secretary of State; the Earl of Chesterfield, and Lord Bolingbroke, a man of great ability, a statesman, a philosopher and an infidel.[1]

Seldom in England's history did a gospel preacher stand before so distinguished, fastidious, and critical an audience.

Whitefield testified, "I go with fear and trembling, knowing how difficult it is to speak to the great so as to win them to Jesus Christ. But divine grace is sufficient for me." We visualize him as he came before this company, weak in himself, but strong in the assurance of being sent of God and of standing as His ambassador. He was also aware of the spiritual need of his hearers, for despite their wealth, many of them were in bondage to the habits of sin, and some were enfeebled by age and soon to leave the bounds of time and enter upon eternity. His words flowed forth with melting compassion as he proclaimed the "good tidings of great joy" — the gospel of Jesus Christ.

His message was planned to reach the intellect first, and after lodging certain basic truths there, to arouse the emotion and move the will.

Lord Bolingbroke, after hearing him for the first time, came to him and declared that he "had done great justice to the divine attributes." And in a later letter to Lady Huntingdon he stated,

Mr Whitefield is the most extraordinary man of our times. He has the most commanding eloquence I ever heard in any person; his abilities are very considerable — his zeal unquenchable and his piety and excellence genuine. . . .[2]

Likewise the Earl of Chesterfield, himself a renowned orator, declared,

Mr Whitefield's eloquence is unrivalled—his zeal inexhaustible; and not to admire both would argue a total absence of taste. . . .[3]

The Earl of Bath, one of the most powerful Parliamentary figures of the century, after hearing Whitefield for the first time, came to him greatly moved and arranged that he visit him. Following that visit, the Earl associated himself with the company that met regularly at Lady Huntingdon's. Similarly, Lord St. John became a believer under Whitefield's preaching. But he shortly passed from earth, and Lady Huntingdon, following his victorious death, in a letter to Whitefield remarked, "This, my good friend, is the firstfruits of that plenteous harvest which, I trust, the great Harvestman will yet reap amongst the nobility of our land."[4]

Under Whitefield's ministry Lady Chesterfield also experienced a changed heart and a transformed life. She was "one of the finest private musicians of her day" and was the friend of such men as Handel and Giardini. But she willingly forsook her association with high society and bore the reproach of the world because of her testimony to Christ. The last time she attended the Royal Court she was wearing a dress brought by Lord Chesterfield from abroad. But the King came to her and remarked, "I know who chose that gown for you—Mr Whitefield. I hear you have attended on him this year and a half." To which she replied, "Yes, I have, and I like him very much." He walked away, but she would have liked to say more.

Whitefield's influence reached into the royal family, particularly in the person of Frederick, the Prince of Wales. But when the prince had been under gospel influence for some two years he was overtaken by death. Lady Huntingdon stated, "He had frequent argument with my Lord Bolingbroke, who thought his Royal Highness fast verging toward Methodism. . . . The Prince went more than once privately to hear Mr Whitefield, with whom he was much pleased."[5]

David Hume, widely-known today for his agnosticism, was also one of Whitefield's hearers. Hume declared, "Mr Whitefield is the most ingenious preacher I ever heard. It is worth going twenty miles to hear him." He also reported that as Whitefield was closing one of his sermons,

He then, in the most simple but energetic language, described what he called the Saviour's dying love to sinful man, so that almost the whole assembly was melted into tears. This address was accompanied with such animated yet natural action that it surpassed anything I ever saw or heard in any preacher.[6]

Whitefield also sought to influence various of the aristocracy by writing to them. For instance to Lord Rae, a military officer, he stated, "Can I wish your Lordship anything greater than that you may be a good soldier of Jesus Christ? It is a blessed thing to be engaged in fighting his battles." Likewise to Colonel Gumley, father-in-law to Lord Bath, he wrote, "The news of your conversion hath reached the ears of many of the great ones in Scotland. May the Lord Jesus keep you steadfast, unmoveable, always abounding in his work." And in reply to a letter received from a countess, Whitefield said, "Your letter speaks the language of a soul which has tasted that the Lord is good, and hath been initiated into the Divine life. Welcome, honoured Madam, into the world of new creatures."

Lady Huntingdon conducted a steady witness for Christ among these titled acquaintances. She was a born leader and at times proved inflexible, but she was also a gracious and humble Christian. Moreover, she had come into clear doctrinal convictions, embracing a Calvinism like that of Whitefield. Her belief is evident in a letter she wrote to the Rev. Henry Venn, who had manifested an uncertain concept of "the doctrines of grace." Her letter reads,

O, my friend! we can make no atonement to a violated law — we have no inward holiness of our own — the Lord Jesus is the Lord our righteousness.

Cling not to such beggarly elements — such filthy rags — mere cob webs of Pharisaical pride — but look to him who hath wrought out a perfect righteousness for his people.

You find it a hard task to come naked and miserable to Christ. . . . But if you come at all you must come thus. . . . There must be no conditions — Christ and Christ alone must be the only Mediator between God and sinful men — no miserable performances may be placed between the sinner and the Saviour. Let the eye of faith be ever directed to the Lord Jesus Christ; and I beseech him to bring every thought of your heart into captivity to the obedience of our great High Priest.[7]

Two of the great ladies, after hearing Whitefield in a certain chapel, assured Lady Huntingdon he had declared that the love of

Christ for sinners was so strong "he would accept even the devil's castaways." The ladies questioned the wisdom of his statement, and therefore Lady Huntingdon brought them to him and asked about the matter. He replied that it was true, but went on to report that following that utterance an elderly woman had called on him and had told him she was passing the door of the chapel when she heard him say, "Christ would receive even the devil's castaways." "Such," she confessed, "am I. Do you think He will receive me?" Whitefield assured her He would if she was but willing to go to Him. This interview ended in a thorough conversion, and Lady Huntingdon discovered that this poor woman's life thereafter was remarkable for its purity and that at her death she left a clear testimony that Christ had indeed washed away her crimson stains.

Whitefield's ministry was well-suited to the colliers of Kingswood and the slaves of America, and yet he equally influenced such minds as Franklin and Belcher in America, and Bolingbroke, Chesterfield, and indeed this company of the learned and dignified, the aristocracy, in England.

Though long by following multitudes admired,
No party for himself he e'er desired;
His one desire to make the Saviour known,
To magnify the name of Christ alone:
If others strove who should the greatest be,
No lover of preeminence was he,
Nor envied those his Lord vouchsafed to bless,
But joyed in theirs as in his own success.

Charles Wesley
An Elegy on the Late Rev George Whitefield
1770

19

"Let Me Be But the Servant of All"

*D*espite Whitefield's declaration that he would no longer act as moderator of the Calvinistic Methodist Association, as we have seen, several of the Societies refused to accept that resignation. These were composed chiefly of men and women who had been converted under his ministry, and their affection for him was unmovable. They continued to regard him as their leader and to declare themselves his people.

Accordingly, although he did not form any new Societies, a loving fellowship was maintained between himself and the Societies that already existed. Yet he gave no direct leadership to them as a movement, but left them to manage their own affairs.

In his ongoing labors, however, Whitefield assisted evangelical efforts in all denominations.

His loyalty remained basically with the Church of England. "The principles that I maintain," he asserted, "are every way agreeable to the Church of England Articles." And to a clergyman who denied the doctrine of "justification by faith" he declared, "This is the doctrine of the Church of England. Unless you hold this and other evangelical principles, how, dear Sir, is it consistent with sincerity to eat her bread?"

Whitefield not only preached the great doctrines of evangelical Christianity himself, but he sought to influence other clergymen to believe and preach them too. In 1741 he had addressed,

> . . . a word of exhortation to my dear brethren . . . whom God shall stir up to go forth into the highways and hedges, into the lanes and streets, to compel poor sinners to come in. . . . O my brethren, have compassion

on our dear Lord's Church, which He has purchased with His own blood. Suffer none of them to be as sheep having no shepherd, or worse than none, those blind leaders of the blind who let them perish for lack of knowledge.

Whitefield declared that despite being ordained by a bishop, no man can be a true minister of Jesus Christ without being born again. He likewise urged all ministers not to be satisfied with preaching on Sundays only, but to do so seven days a week; to preach in the open air and not to be limited to their own parishes, but to go forth wherever lost souls were found and to proclaim the grace of God to them. Such actions, he assured them, would bring the opposition of authorities and the hatred of the world, but it would also witness the blessing of God.

As the years passed, several new evangelical men were raised up in the Church of England, and when in 1755 Whitefield arrived home from his fifth visit to America he stated, "Glad am I to hear that so many have lately been stirred up to preach a crucified Saviour. Surely that Scripture must be fulfilled, 'And many of the priests were obedient to the word.'" There were also several outstanding laymen who were sound in the faith and bold in maintaining their testimony.

Certain of these clergymen had been converted without human instrumentality, and their lives are a remarkable evidence that salvation is a work of God. But we may be sure that since Whitefield, the Wesleys, and Lady Huntingdon were all members of the Church of England and were seeking to advance the Church's work, these clergymen were subject to their influence in regard to evangelical principles.

Moreover, these evangelical clergymen and laymen were virtually all Calvinists. We notice such names as Daniel Rowland and Howell Davies of Wales, George Thompson and Samuel Walker of Cornwall, William Romaine and Martin Madan of London, John Berridge and Thomas Haweis of the Midlands, and William Grimshaw and Henry Venn of Yorkshire. Among the laymen were Lord Dartmouth, commemorated in the college that bears his name in America, John Thornton, who had amassed great wealth in the export trade, and James Ireland, a highly successful wool merchant. Because of "the doctrines of grace" to which they all held, between these men and Whitefield and Lady Huntingdon there was warm fellowship. These men also respected Wesley for the abundance of his work, but in most cases the fellowship was less familiar.

Whitefield had given up the leading of Calvinistic Methodism, but now the Evangelical Party within the Church of England had developed, and his example had been an important factor in bringing it about. All of Christianity is indebted to the Evangelical Party in the Church of England for its scholarship, its contribution to Christian hymnology, and its activities in foreign missions.

Whitefield rendered service also to the Wesleys. This was most notable in his preventing, in the words of Nehemiah Curnock, the editor of John Wesley's *Journals*, "a breach between John and Charles Wesley . . . which must . . . either have rent the Methodist Society in twain, or, more probably, have scattered it to the winds."[1]

In 1749 Charles Wesley had married. His bride was Sarah Gwynne, daughter of Marmaduke Gwynne, a man of substance and authority, residing at Garth House, a mansion in south Wales. Gwynne had been converted under the ministry of Howell Harris, and by that association he came to know the Wesleys. Sarah proved a gracious and talented wife, and Charles's married life knew great happiness.

A few months later John Wesley determined that he too should marry. In Newcastle, Yorkshire John had founded a school and an orphanage, and one of its chief workers was an attractive young widow, Mrs. Grace Murray. Mrs. Murray was also an earnest Christian and a woman of much prayer, and many Methodists testified to her tenderness and the help she gave in times of trouble.

During 1748 John Bennet, one of Wesley's most capable young preachers, becoming sick, came under Mrs. Murray's care. He came from a well-to-do family, had trained as a lawyer, and, being accepted as one of Wesley's lay preachers, preached with conviction. The anointing of God was manifestly upon him, and he founded several Societies.

Bennet remained under Mrs. Murray's care for five months. They were each about thirty-three at the time. A vital friendship sprang up between them, and before he left the institution they were engaged to be married.

But John Wesley shortly fell sick, and he too came under Mrs. Murray's care. She thought she had been in love with Bennet, but now that Wesley was near she felt she was in love with him.

Moreover, Wesley was equally fond of her, and when he was better he took her with him on evangelistic trips. While in Ireland they entered into an arrangement known as a *spousal de praesenti*; this meant that they were in effect married, but the consummation would come later following the marriage ceremony.

Upon returning to Bristol, Mrs. Murray heard tales to the effect that Wesley was showing affection to another woman, and she turned again to Bennet. Yet when she met Wesley again she declared she "wanted to live and die with him," and he planned to complete the marriage as soon as he had informed his brother and the Methodist people.

But Charles Wesley was convinced that, excellent woman though she was, Grace Murray was not of sufficient standing to marry a Wesley. He also felt that John was using his position to take her away from Bennet, and he determined to prevent such a deed from taking place. In his impetuous nature he rode posthaste to the north of England where Grace was staying, put her on the horse behind him, and rode to find Bennet. Charles then saw to it that the two were married the following morning.

John shortly arrived at Leeds. Realizing he had lost Grace Murray, probably the only true love of his life, he was heartbroken. He reported,

> Mr Whitefield wept and prayed over me . . . he said all that was in his power to comfort me, but it was in vain. . . . My brother came. . . . I felt no anger, yet I did not desire to see him. But Mr Whitefield constrained me. After a few words had passed he [Charles] accosted me with, 'I renounce all intercourse with you, but what I would have with an heathen man or a publican.' . . . Poor Mr Whitefield and John Nelson [one of Wesley's preachers] burst into tears. They prayed, cried and entreated till the storm passed away.[2]

At last Charles Wesley's severe opposition was overcome, and the breach was prevented. Wesleyan Methodism was saved from what would have been a disastrous division, and this was due, as Dr. Curnock states, "to the tact and tenderness of Whitefield and Nelson."

Whitefield also preached for the Wesleys in several of their Societies. After he had ministered in their Room at Newcastle John stated, "I am now satisfied that God sent Mr Whitefield thither in an acceptable time, many of those who had little thought of God before still retaining the impressions they received from him." And after he devoted some days to their Society in Leeds Charles reported, "The door has remained open ever since Mr Whitefield preached here, and quite removed the prejudices of our first opposers. Some of them were convinced by him and some converted and added to the church."

And of the first occasion of his preaching at the Foundery in London Whitefield stated, "I preached to a very crowded and affected auditory. Mr Wesley read prayers. On Sunday I read prayers and he preached. The sacrament was administered to about twelve hundred."

Wesley's people in Ireland were suffering great violence, and Whitefield used his association with the aristocracy to have the matter brought before the King, seeking relief for them. He also went to Ireland himself — the visit of 1751 — and although Wesley's work was struggling when he arrived, when he left it was much revived. A hearer, one who held Wesley's beliefs, remarked,

> What blessed seasons have we had since Mr Whitefield came. Thousands constantly attended the word. I never heard a man preach holiness of heart in a clearer manner. He powerfully preaches Christ for us and in us. I confess I had strange ideas about him, but blessed be God, I have not now.[3]

In 1753, Wesley was in London and became sick. He proved dangerously ill with consumption — so much so that he wrote his own epitaph. Charles hastened up to London to be with him. Whitefield also immediately set out for London, but he wrote to John, and his letter reveals his depth of affection:

> . . . A radiant throne awaits you, and ere long you will enter into your Master's joy. . . . If prayers can detain . . . even you, reverend and very dear Sir, shall not leave us yet. . . . But if you must now fall asleep in Jesus, may . . . you die in the embrace of triumphant love. . . . May underneath you be Christ's everlasting arms! I commend you to his never-failing mercy. . . .

But John recovered from this illness, and there lay before him nearly forty years of labor for the Lord.

In 1756 Charles Wesley stated,

I rejoiced to hear of the great good Mr Whitefield has done in our Societies. . . . He did his utmost to strengthen our hands and deserves the thanks of all the churches for his abundant labour of love.[4]

Whitefield went on in this manner, as "the servant of all," year after year. Following his death in 1770 Thomas Olivers, one of Wesley's most capable preachers, declared,

While Mr Whitefield lived he was glad to confirm his love to the members of Wesley's Societies, by preaching in their chapels, sitting at their tables, lying in their beds, by conversing with them late and early, in the most friendly manner.

When he preached in Mr Wesley's pulpits . . . multitudes can tell what expressions of the highest esteem he frequently made use of. . . . When he had opportunity he gladly attended our Conferences. . . . He often said such things on our behalf as modesty forbids me to mention.[5]

During any year that he was in England Whitefield made a visit to Scotland, and although on some of the final ones he was very weak, he nevertheless forced himself to preach, thus assisting the Evangelicals of that land.

In 1757, however, he went from Scotland to Ireland. Great crowds heard him in Dublin, but before long,

. . . on Sunday afternoon, after preaching in Oxmantown-green, a place frequented by the Ormon and Liberty boys, who often fight there, he narrowly escaped with his life.

In the time of sermon and prayer a few stones were thrown at him, which did no hurt. But when he had done and thought to return home the way he came, access was denied, and he was obliged to go near a half a mile through hundreds of papists. Finding him unattended, for a soldier and four preachers who came with him had fled, they threw vollies of stones upon him from all quarters, and made him reel backwards and forwards, till he was almost breathless, and all over a gore of blood.

At last, with great difficulty, he staggered to the door of a preacher's house which was kindly opened to him. For a while he continued speechless and panting for breath; but his weeping friends having given him some cordials and washed his wounds [were afraid their house would be attacked]. A coach was procured, in which, amidst the oaths, imprecations and threatenings of the rabble, he got safe to his lodgings.

He then joined in a hymn of thanksgiving with his friends. Next morning he set out for Port Arlington, 'leaving' he says, 'my persecutors to His mercy, who of persecutors has often made preachers. I pray God I may thus be revenged of them.'[6]

He remained in Ireland for another three weeks and remarked, "Everywhere the glorious *Emmanuel* smiled upon my labours," and in these efforts he largely assisted the work of the Wesleys.

In his labors in America Whitefield had endeavored, as we have seen, to be in attendance at a Church of England each Sunday morning. But being so ill-treated by Commissary Garden, he forsook this practice in the Southern Colonies, yet largely continued it when further north.

His assistance, however, was welcomed by men of various denominations who were sound in the faith. He worked with the Independents (Congregationalists) in New England, with the Baptists in Rhode Island and elsewhere, and with the Presbyterians in the Middle Colonies. In all these efforts he was simply preaching the gospel which was believed by these several pastors.

Whitefield made not the least effort to bind the numerous people whom he reached in an allegiance to himself. He went among them to assist any evangelical minister, and although the tremendous opportunity was available to establish a lasting and organized relationship, he had no desire to do so. And he went on in this manner during his several visits to America.

Nonetheless, late in life he realized that there were numerous people who had been touched by his ministry, but who were not now reached by any church. Many of these were in newly-developed areas remote from all religious organizations, and in a letter to John Wesley he stated, "The Gospel range is of such large extent that I have, as it were, scarce begun to begin. . . . Here is room for a hundred itinerants. Lord Jesus, send by whom thou wilt send!"[7] And when Whitefield was on his final voyage across the Atlantic, Wesley's first two overseas itinerants, Richard Boardman and Joseph Pilmoor, were also on the ocean, on their way to establish Wesleyan Methodist

Societies — the first of a host that were later to follow in the broad expanses of the New World.

For the last almost twenty years of his life, in England and Wales, in Scotland and Ireland, and in all the Colonies of America, by aiding all who were sound in the faith Whitefield put his enunciated principle into effect: "I want to be but the servant of all!"

For friendship form'd by nature and by grace
(His heart made up of truth and tenderness,)
Stranger to guile, unknowing to deceive,
In anger, malice or revenge to live,
He lived, himself on others to bestow
A ministerial spirit here below,
Beloved by all the lovers of the Lord,
By none but Satan's synagogue abhorred.

Charles Wesley
An Elegy on the Late Rev George Whitefield
1770

20

Associates

*W*hitefield's life went on in the way in which it had begun. He turned neither to the right nor to the left, and only while physically invalided did he pause in his incredible program of labor. During each year that he was in England he made a trip to Scotland, and yet another four times he visited America.

Instead, however, of looking into all these activities individually, we will seek to learn of his career by looking at the lives of certain of his associates.

Charles Wesley

For sixteen years Charles labored with unfailing zeal as an open-air preacher. He was fearless in his declaration of the gospel. His word went forth with power. He faced mobs with boldness, lived virtually a homeless life, and, above all, was used of God in the winning of numerous souls to Jesus Christ. He was the constant partner of his brother in the founding and upbuilding of Methodist Societies.

By 1750 Charles had experienced certain changes in his theological thought. As we have seen, he no longer fully believed John's teaching of sinless perfection, and he now accepted to some extent the doctrine of predestination.[1] In 1752 he wrote to Whitefield suggesting he might throw in his lot with him. But Whitefield replied, "The connection between you and your brother hath been so close and your attachment to him so necessary to keep up his interest that I would not, for the world, do or say anything that may separate such friends."[2]

Three years later Charles addressed an "Epistle" to Whitefield, declaring there was no longer any barrier between them. It begins,

Come on, my Whitefield! (since the strife is past,
And friends at first are friends again at last). . . .

While Charles was a mighty evangelist, he was also a powerful poet, and it is in that regard that he is most remembered today. He composed just under nine thousand poems, most of which are hymns, and he is undoubtedly the greatest of all English hymn-writers. Following Whitefield's death, Charles penned in verse a picture of his life, *An Elegy*, a work of 536 lines, several selections from which are cited in this book.

John Cennick

We saw that when Whitefield sailed the third time to America, he placed John Cennick in the superintendency of his Societies and of the Tabernacle. Cennick was a truly godly man and a very capable preacher, but he proved too gentle to handle the problems that arose. He felt the need of strong associates, and since he loved the Moravians he went over to their movement.

He became a Moravian missionary in Ireland. Renting an unused church in Dublin, he

. . . preached twice daily to crowds so great that those who wished to hear must be present two or three hours before the time. . . . All the windows were taken down so that people might hear in the burying-ground and environs, yet multitudes were disappointed. . . . Often seven or eight priests were together to hear him, and many of the Church clergy. . . .[3]

In Cennick's congregation there was a capable young preacher, Benjamin La Trobe. (His son, of the same name, was a chief architect in the reconstruction of the Capitol Building in Washington, D.C. in 1819.) Cennick left La Trobe to conduct the work in Dublin, while he accepted the many invitations he had received to minister in northern Ireland.

He held meetings in barns, houses, and fields and for many months was subject to bitter persecution — beaten by hoodlums, set upon by dogs, attacked by mobs, and arrested and fined. He and his wife were often in utter poverty, but his joy in the Lord abounded. He was patient and kind, and people saw in him a Christianity that was beautiful and real. As a result,

He was loved . . . by all classes and by all denominations. At Moneymore the Presbyterians asked him to be their minister. At Ballynahone the Roman Catholics said if he would only settle there they would never go to mass again. At New Mills the people rushed from their cabins, barred his way, offered him milk, and besought him saying, 'If you cannot stop to preach, at least come into our house to pray.' . . . He was so beloved that many of the inn-keepers gave him board and lodging free of charge. . . . The parish priest at Balinderry wished, he said, he had the privilege of accompanying Cennick on his journeys. He would pocket the money and drink the liquor that Cennick refused.[4]

In the space of seven years, Cennick established forty Societies and built no fewer than ten churches.

We see something of Cennick's spirit in a letter he wrote to a fellow-pastor who seemed to feel there was some slight difference between them. Cennick wrote,

. . . My heart is as your heart, and Jesus shall still be the faithful witness between us, that we will aim at nothing in all our love and correspondence, but to live and act for his Name's sake. He is the God of our life, the Angel that saved us out of the world . . . and whose presence shall be our most precious treasure forever. The best blessing He has, light upon thee, keep thee in peace and in true poverty; and in all thy labours, His ears be open to thy sighs, and his hand lead thee till I kiss thee above![5]

Cennick was a gifted poet. From him we have the Grace before meals ("Be present at our table, Lord") and the hymns "Jesus my all to heaven is gone," "Children of the heavenly King," "Thou dear redeemer, dying Lamb," and numerous others. "Lo He comes with clouds descending" is largely from his pen. He died at the age of thirty-six, and in his pocket was found a poem, *"Nunc Dimittis"* — verses which breathe a beautiful spirit of calm resignation to the will of God, an unquestioning assurance of Heaven, and a deep longing to be there. It would be greatly to the welfare of Christians everywhere if he were more widely-known.

Howell Harris

From almost the very week of his conversion in 1735 Harris preached daily and often two or three times a day, with discourses that lasted an hour and frequently more. For years he was constantly on the go, preaching at fairs and wakes, declaring the gospel to multitudes in the open air and visiting Societies.[6] And repeatedly for months at a stretch he bore the oversight of Whitefield's work in London. He had no definite income and often went without adequate food; yet when he received a gift of money, he invariably gave a considerable portion to the poor.

His zeal was amazing. He made, for instance, such reports as, "To the Tabernacle to preach. Satan raged a little in his servants, and God strengthened me inwardly accordingly. There was a great crowd. I did so sweat that I was all wet through my clothes, and so spent that I could hardly walk."[7] "Discoursed on . . . the glory of the word COME. I had such power and voice clear, calling, threatening and beating the desk, so that I felt I was in the suburbs of heaven." "Came home past 2 [A.M.] having travelled this week near 250 miles being sorely tired and worn out, I and my horse."

After a visit to North Wales to encourage a group of persecuted believers he wrote, "I have now visited . . . 13 Counties and travaild mostly 150 miles a Week and discoursed twice every day & sometimes three and four times a day & this last Journey I have not taken off my Cloaths for 7 Nights and travaild from one morning to ye next morning on ye Mountain, being obliged to meet at that time by Reason of Persecution."[8]

Moreover, during his days in north Wales, while holding an open-air meeting in the town of Bala, Harris received, he says, ". . . a blow on the head with violence enough to slit my head in two."

A man in the best of health could ill have stood the exertions that were constant in Harris's life, and it appears that the blow on the head brought a change in his procedure. At least he now became somewhat irresponsible, this condition being manifest chiefly in that he began to allow himself to be governed by a Mrs. Sydney Griffith.

In 1748 Madame Griffith left her husband, a drunken squire, and was taken by Harris (with his wife's consent) into his home. She was twenty-nine, a woman of some personal strength and physical attractiveness, and he believed she possessed the apostolic gift of prophecy. He took her with him on his evangelistic journeys and accepted her judgments for and against spiritual leaders in Wales.

Christians were appalled at this behavior, and many ceased all cooperation with Harris. Moreover, he soon went to London,

Madame Griffith followed him, and he came to Whitefield expecting to preach at the Tabernacle. Of course Whitefield refused him.
Harris reported that Whitefield said "he did not approve of Madam
Griffith being with me, that it was contrary to God's word, and
spake with great authority in his spirit."[9] Madame Griffith, however, soon died.

Harris settled down at his home at Trevecca in Wales. Several of his
followers, in order to be near him, came there too, and he began enlarg-
ing his house till it became a kind of community institution. He was
often, however, very unwell, and his mind frequently seemed unbal-
anced. After some years he improved to some extent and sought out
Whitefield and the Wesleys, and they received him. He also began to
preach again, but never regained the force and fervor of his former
years.

Our sympathies go out to Howell Harris, a most sincere man who
overworked himself in seeking to serve the Lord.

Benjamin Franklin

Benjamin Franklin was one of the most discerning of men. We saw
that when Whitefield first arrived in Philadelphia Franklin took particular notice of him, reported on the effects of his ministry, estimated
that he could be heard by thirty thousand people, and complimented
his oratorical powers.

Upon beginning his next visit to America Whitefield was unwell,
and Franklin, learning soon of some improvement, wrote, "I am glad
to hear Mr Whitefield . . . has recovered his health. He is a good man,
and I love him."[10] Whitefield shortly preached a sermon expressing
his delight that the Jacobite Rebellion in England had been put down.
Franklin reported, "No discourse of his among us has given more
general satisfaction; nor has the Preacher ever met with more universal applause, having demonstrated himself to be as sound and zealous
a Protestant . . . as he is a good and masterly orator."[11]

And on an occasion when Whitefield was leaving Philadelphia,
Franklin stated, as we have seen, "Mr Whitefield was never so generally well esteemed by persons of all ranks among us; nor did he
ever leave us with so many ardent wishes for a safe return."[12]

Franklin indicated the relation between Whitefield and himself by
reporting:

The following statement will show something of the terms on which we stood. Upon one of his arrivals from England, he wrote to me that he should soon come to Philadelphia, but knew not where he should lodge when there. . . . My answer was 'You know my house; if you can make shift with its scanty accommodations, you will be most heartily welcome.' He replied, that if I made that kind offer for Christ's sake, I should not miss of a reward. And I returned, 'Don't let me be mistaken, it was not for Christ's sake, but for yours.'[13]

From Franklin's correspondence we find that his mother-in-law, Mrs. Read, was a regular contributor to the Orphan House, and that on one occasion his sister-in-law "entertained several friends" by reading them the account of Whitefield's activities contained in a letter from Franklin.

When Franklin learned that Whitefield was preaching regularly to the nobility in England, he wrote to him, saying, "I am glad to hear that you have frequent opportunities of preaching among the great. If you can gain them to a good and exemplary life, wonderful changes will follow in the manners of the lower ranks. . . ."[14] He closed his letter with the words, "My wife and family join in the most cordial salutations to you and good Mrs Whitefield. I am, dear Sir, your very affectionate friend. . . ."

In 1740 Franklin conceived the idea of founding an academy in Philadelphia and using as its headquarters the auditorium that had been built for Whitefield to preach in. He wrote to Whitefield asking for suggestions as to the curriculum and organization of the proposed institution, and Whitefield replied: ". . . Your plan I have read over, and do not wonder as to its meeting general approbation. It is certainly well calculated to promote polite literature; but I think there wants *aliquid Christi* [something of Christ] in it. . . ."[15] Whitefield went on to state that Christianity is the foundation on which arts and science should be built, to suggest the need of adequate teachers, and also to suggest his hearty agreement with the entire project.

A further letter from Franklin suggested that the two of them should unite in a new and history-making undertaking. It reads:

I sometimes wish that you and I were jointly employed by the Crown to settle a Colony in Ohio. . . . What a glorious thing it would be to settle in that fine Country a large Strong body of Religious and Industrious

people. . . . Might it not generally facilitate the Introduction of pure
Religion among the Heathen, if we could by such a Colony, show them
a better Sample of Christians than they commonly see in our Indian
Traders? . . . In such an enterprise I could spend the Remainder of my
life with pleasure; and I firmly believe God would bless us with
success. . . .[16]

Accordingly, it is evident Franklin was not always the agnostic he
is believed to have been.

In 1766 Franklin was in England, where on behalf of the American
Colonies he effected a vigorous opposition to the Stamp Act. Franklin
was examined in the matter before the House of Commons, and
Whitefield, who was present, reported: "Dr Franklin has gained
immortal honour by his behaviour at the bar of the House. . . . He stood
unappalled, gave pleasure to his friends, and did honour to his country."

Certain Americans, however, mistakenly felt that Franklin had
betrayed his country, and therefore a company of his friends planned
to publish an account of his statements. Joseph Galloway, a prominent Pennsylvania lawyer, in writing to Franklin's son, declared that
Whitefield's name must be included among those defending Franklin,
asserting, "It will certainly put an effectual stop to the malignant lies
concerning Mr F's conduct relating to the Stamp Act. . . . For who
would dare deny Mr Whitefield's authority — will the Church? Will
the Presbyterians?"

Whitefield died in 1770, and Franklin wrote, "I knew him inti-
mately upwards of 30 years. His integrity, disinterestedness and indefatigable zeal in prosecuting every good work, I have never seen
equalled and shall never see excelled."[17]

Late in life Franklin wrote an account of his relationships with
Whitefield. By that time, however, his own standards of behavior had
changed to some extent, and, perhaps as a salve for his conscience,
he criticized the literary efforts of his friend for whom he had previously had only praise. Moreover, he also stated, "Mr Whitefield used
to pray for my conversion but never had the satisfaction of feeling
that his prayers were heard." Perhaps herein lies the cause of his
change.

Whitefield's only calculation in the construction of a building was, how many immortal souls could be crowded within four square walls and under a roof to hear 'the joyful sound.'

Ah, but when I consider that every stone in the Tottenham Court Road Chapel has echoed to the sound of salvation and the hymns of redeemed spirits, and that almost every spot on the floor has been moistened by tears of repentance . . . there comes over me an awe and solemnity which no modern gothic structure with its lofty arches and painted windows can inspire.

Joseph Belcher
George Whitefield: A Biography
c. 1850

21

Building for God

A lthough Whitefield had declared he would no longer serve as the head of Calvinistic Methodism, the people would not let him go. They would accept as pastor of the Tabernacle no one but himself, and therefore he continued in that office, preaching to the crowds that attended and overseeing its several functions — this besides ministering throughout Britain and making his several visits to America.

In 1753, however, he was faced with the need to replace the Tabernacle with a new and more permanent structure.

The memories of the old place were many and precious. At the time of its construction (1741) it had provided Whitefield with a meeting-house and a headquarters. Here he had brought his bride and introduced her to his congregation, and here both Harris and Cennick had exercised months of mighty ministry. And here, during whatever weeks he was in London, Whitefield had preached, witnessing much of the power of God upon his ministry and the conversion of large numbers of sinners.

The need for a new building was made all the more acute by the extraordinary measure of blessing that accompanied his ministry in 1752. He said, "The glory of the Lord fills the Tabernacle. We hear every day of persons brought under fresh awakenings. . . . We have had two most awful sacraments."

Accordingly he had plans drawn up for a new Tabernacle. Within a few weeks he had received more than £1000. He then laid the first brick, and construction was begun. And while the work was going on, he launched out on a preaching circuit "of seven hundred miles."

The Tabernacle was eighty feet square and of double brick construction. The account of the opening services reads, "The

Tabernacle, though capable with its surrounding galleries, of containing about four thousand people, was crowded almost to suffocation, in every part; and there . . . the Lord made manifest by this apostolic man . . . the savour of his grace."

Dr. John Byrom, the father of English shorthand and author of the hymn "Christians awake, salute the happy morn," tells of being at Lady Huntingdon's with Colonel Gumley and Whitefield. He goes on to say,

> The Colonel, Mr Whitefield and myself came away in a coach that Lady Huntingdon provided. The Colonel took leave of us at Hyde Park Corner, and I went on with Mr Whitefield to the Tabernacle. . . .
>
> Mr Whitefield went up and gave them a sermon, and got me a seat just behind him, and afterwards invited me to supper in his apartments which are just by.
>
> And so I had opportunity of talking with this remarkable youth, which I never had before, and a very extraordinary one he is. . . . His Tabernacle will hold 3000 people, and it seemed to be quite full.[1]

Whitefield also assisted the singing in the Tabernacle by compiling a new hymnbook, *Hymns for Social Worship*, "designed for the use of the Tabernacle congregation."

Throughout many years following Whitefield's death the Tabernacle had a succession of godly pastors, and the "doctrines of grace" formed the basis of their ministries. Among the young men in attendance were R. W. Dale, who became a noted theologian, and John Williams, the martyr-missionary to Erromanga in the South Seas.

After serving for 116 years the building was replaced by a smaller structure, a stone building at the corner of Leonard and Tabernacle Streets. It stands today and is used as a gymnasium for a nearby school.

Likewise many of the people in Bristol refused to relinquish their relation with Whitefield, and they continued to regard themselves as "a Whitefield Society." They met in a hall that was formerly a monastery refectory.

Lady Huntingdon had a home in a Bristol suburb, and in 1749 she began soliciting funds for the construction of a Tabernacle there. Lord and Lady Chesterfield were donors, as was also the Earl of Bath. The Earl wrote,

It gives me unfeigned pleasure to hear of the good effects of Mr Whitefield's ministry. . . . I feel indebted to your Ladyship for an opportunity of contributing to so good a cause, firmly persuaded that the finger of an unerring Providence will point out some other and far distant lands . . . where the ministrations of our excellent friend . . . shall perform those mighty deeds which shall overwhelm generations, yet unborn, with gratitude to the kind Author of all our mercies. . . .[2]

The Bristol Tabernacle was built in a fashionable district on Penn Street. Whitefield reported, "On Sunday I opened the new Tabernacle. It is large, but not half large enough: would the place contain them I believe near as many would come as in London."[3]

We have seen that Whitefield and Cennick built their own schoolhouse after Wesley seized the former one. It stands today, and various visitors to Bristol have assumed it is Whitefield's Bristol Tabernacle. The Tabernacle, however, was in a different area and was much larger. It served more than a century before it was dismantled.

In London during 1755 Whitefield experienced the most sustained opposition of his entire career.

He was offered the use of a Dissenting meeting-house, the Long Acre Chapel. He had long desired to reach the district in which it was situated with the gospel, and therefore he began to preach in the chapel twice a week.

But while he preached within, a violent uproar was made without. A rabble making as much noise as possible constantly surrounded the building, and some men went so far as to construct a platform on an adjacent property from which they created pandemonium during each service.

The opposition arose to some extent from the theatre people, but there was also another cause. War had recently broken out with France, the French intended to replace King George with a monarch of their own choice, and several Englishmen were in agreement with the plan. Indeed, at this time the landing of a French force on the shores of England was daily expected. In the midst of these circumstances Whitefield published *A Short Address to Persons of All Denominations*, "Occasioned by the Alarm of an Intended Invasion." It declared his own loyalty to the crown and endeavored to arouse strong support for England and the King. The pamphlet drew vigorous commendations, even from some who had formerly opposed him, but it also put added venom to the attack being made on him in Long Acre.

After publishing the *Address*, Whitefield received three anonymous letters threatening him with assassination. He took the matter to the legal authorities, who in turn brought it before the King. His Majesty issued an official announcement offering a reward for information as to the perpetrator

Because of the pronounced hostility, Whitefield decided it would not be possible to do a permanent work at Long Acre. His services there, however, had gathered a large and steady congregation, and he determined to build a meeting-house in which they could assemble. He obtained a location sufficiently distant — a rural property on Tottenham Court Road — and immediately began to build a large chapel.

The building was 70 feet by 127, apparently had two galleries on each of three sides, and was undoubtedly the largest nonestablishment church anywhere in the world.

He and Mrs. Whitefield continued to live at Tabernacle House, but behind the new chapel he built a residence for a minister and twelve almshouses that were allotted without charge to poor widows.

Beneath the Chapel were vaults for the burial of the dead. Whitefield planned that he and Mrs. Whitefield and the pastors of the Chapel should be buried there. But he also wanted the vault to be a symbol of his union with the Wesleys. Wesley's headquarters was still the former cannon factory, and Whitefield told his people,

> I have prepared a vault in this Chapel, where I intend to be buried, and Messrs. John and Charles Wesley shall also be buried there. We will all lie together. You will not let them enter your chapel while they are alive. They can do you no harm when they are dead.[4]

The majority of the people who had attended at Long Acre now attended the Chapel, as did also a number of the nobility who had attended the services in Lady Huntingdon's drawing room. We are told,

> Few places could boast of such a constellation of transcendent genius and senatorial talent, such a brilliant assemblage of wisdom, magnanimity and oratorical powers, as was then to be found within the walls of Tottenham Court and the Tabernacle.[5]

The sculptor John Bacon was a member of the Chapel and manifested his admiration of Whitefield by sculpting a marble likeness of him. The prominent actor Edward Shuter frequently attended, endeavoring to hone his dramatic skills by copying Whitefield. Lord Chesterfield was also often in attendance. On one occasion Whitefield was likening the sinner to an aged and blind beggar being led by his little dog on a cord. He feels his way by tapping on the ground with a cane. But directly before him there lies a great yawning chasm, and as he reaches its edge he loses the dog's leash. The cane falls from his hand, and he lurches forward to retrieve it . . . But at that point Chesterfield, overcome as he visualized the scene, jumped to his feet shouting, "Good God! He's gone! He's gone!"

It must be recognized, however, that by constructing the new Tabernacle and Chapel Whitefield had added to his burdens. Besides the Orphan House in Georgia he now had two large London churches to look after, plus his itinerant ministry in England, Wales, and Scotland, his extensive correspondence, and the great number of persons who constantly came knocking and imploring, "What must I do to be saved?" Yet he carried his burdens in the strength of the Lord, and his sense of victory in Christ ever abounded.

After having stood for a century, the Chapel needed extensive repairs. It was rebuilt, much smaller than it had been; but during the Second World War it was destroyed by enemy action. It was later rebuilt, and although the name over the entrance reads, "The Whitefield Memorial Chapel," the title was changed, and the building now serves as "The American Church in London."

Such for a length of years his glorious race
    He ran, nor e'er look'd back, or slack'd his pace,
Forgetting still the things already done,
    And reaching forth to those not yet begun,
Eager he press'd to his high calling's prize,
    By violent faith resolved to scale the skies,
And apprehend his Lord in paradise.

Charles Wesley
Elegy on the Late Rev George Whitefield
1770

22

"Weary in Thy Work, But Not Weary of It"

*T*he last ten years of Whitefield's life (1760-1770) witnessed a series of events in which, though virtually overcome by physical weakness, upon being confronted by a opportunity to preach he quickly became strong again and declared the Word with both physical and spiritual power. This process characterized the closing decade of his career.

Whitefield had never known vibrantly good health, and as early as 1748 he had given evidence of suffering a definite physical disorder. He was then preaching in Scotland; the weather was boisterous and the wind high, and he became "ill with a hoarseness and a cold in straining to reach large congregations." On his return journey to London he stated, "I am apt to believe I have strained myself inwardly. I feel sensible pain in my breathing."[1]

And this condition did not leave him. From that point onward a distinct weakness was manifest. It seems to have been linked with his "vomiting great quantities of blood" which followed his efforts to make some particularly large congregation hear. In forthcoming months his condition steadily declined, till by 1757, as his first biographer tells us, "his attendance during the winter at both the Chapel and the Tabernacle greatly impaired his health. He was troubled with continual vomitings, got little sleep and had no appetite. Still he went on as well as he could."

During these days, however, an event took place which, among other things, proved he was not out to make gain for himself. A Miss Hunter, a Scottish woman of considerable wealth, made him an offer of her entire estate. This he refused. Then she offered it for the use of the Orphan House, but this also he did not accept. The reasons for his action are not known, but the event is reported and attested by his first biographer, Dr. John Gillies, a Scotsman.[2]

From 1756 onward England was engaged in the Seven Years War with France, and therefore Whitefield had been prevented from making a further visit to America. His passages across the ocean, despite the lack of comfort on board, had provided a measure of relaxation and had proved a physical help. He yearned to sail again, but being retained in England he pursued his labors, ministering at the Chapel and the Tabernacle during the Winter months. Throughout the balance of the year, although he still bore the responsibility of these two works and frequently ministered in their pulpits, he itinerated throughout the British Isles.

Early in 1760, however, Whitefield found himself so weak that he could scarcely preach. He had virtually become an invalid, and he even went to Bristol and tried drinking the supposed health-giving waters there. But all was to no avail. A physician suggested "a perpetual blister," and Whitefield replied, "Give me perpetual preaching."

Nevertheless, despite his condition certain men of the world now made him the particular object of their spite.

A celebrated actor, Samuel Foote, wrote a play entitled *The Minor*[3] and performed it in the Drury Lane Theatre. The play held Whitefield up to obscene ridicule. In mockery of the condition of his eyes it termed him "Dr Squintum"; the other characters were "Shirk," "Shift," and "Mrs Cole." The latter is an old bawd who says, "Mr Whitefield scrubbed me with scouring powder at the Tabernacle and made me clean." She makes loud profession of her conversion, but continues in her vile manner of life. Tyerman says, "The whole thing is steeped in lewdness," and a London magazine remarked, "The satire levelled against the great leader of the Methodists . . . is no less unjust to Mr Whitefield than absurd."[4]

Whitefield made no definite mention of Foote. However, it is possible that he was referring to him when, preaching about Heaven and his longing to be there, he exclaimed, "There, there, the ungodly foot will trample upon the saint no more!"

The Minor was a financial success, and therefore it was both repeated and imitated. Foote performed it in three major theatres, and other writers provided similar productions and staged them in various playhouses. Moreover, several obscene ballads were written about imaginary incidents in Whitefield's life, and numerous lewd tales were circulated about him. It became hardly possible for him to step onto the street without hearing children singing the ballads and older ones taunting him with the false reports.

But as a result of this treatment people came in increasing numbers, crowding into the Tabernacle and the Chapel; and they swelled even more his open-air congregations. In fact, a considerable amount of the opposition Whitefield had long borne died away at this time.

Whitefield undoubtedly suffered inwardly from the vile treatment and the lying reports, but he continued his labors to the fullest of his strength.

Moreover, at this time he assisted certain Christians in Europe. Russia was then at war with Germany, and several German pastors had informed him of their people's suffering under the cruelty of the Cossack soldiers. He appealed to his congregations and received for the Germans' help £450. For this the King of Prussia sent a letter expressing the devout gratitude of himself and his people.

Whitefield's health, however, now became much worse, and in 1761 he was brought to the gates of death. But as soon as he was able he arose from his sickbed, got out of London, and ministered at Bristol and Plymouth. Yet he soon found it necessary to return to London, and there the responsibilities of the Tabernacle and Chapel quickly began to lay him low.

He felt that a sea trip would help, but since the war still prevented a trans-Atlantic voyage, he accepted the invitations he had received to sail to Holland. Although the language difference prevented him from drawing large congregations, he nevertheless preached through an interpreter, and did so in several cities.[5]

Much improved in health after a month in Holland, he returned to England and immediately launched into his labors. While preaching at Norwich he was provided with a "prophet's chamber," and he spoke of "lying on a nasty, stinking mattress, continually bit by fleas."[6] Whitefield was a man of exceptional neatness and cleanliness, and his own home was remarkable for the absence of these pests, then so prevalent in the homes of England.

Late in 1762 the war came to an end, and Whitefield immediately made plans to sail to America. He placed the Chapel and the Tabernacle in the hands of three trustees, able and godly men: Keen, Hardy, and Beckman. He once more visited Scotland — his thirteenth visit — and while there he said, "My poor tabernacle is so far restored as to enable me to mount my Gospel throne once a day. Perhaps the sea air will brace me up a little more." John Wesley was in Scotland at the time and after visiting with him said, "Humanly speaking he is worn out. His frame has received its major shock."

Whitefield reached America — coming for the sixth time — in August 1763. Eight years had passed since his last visit, and he had altered physically. His weariness showed on his countenance, and he had grown somewhat corpulent. But the people welcomed him with excited joy, and as he traveled from the port to Bethesda he said, "All along the cry is 'For Christ's sake, stay and preach to us!'"

The income from the plantation that his friends had provided for the support of the Orphan House allowed him now "to pay off all Bethesda's arrears." He found the residence and the school in the best of order and the grounds beautified, and the place proved to him a joy and contentment.

Whitefield again launched out on an extensive preaching tour.

While in Connecticut he visited a school for Indian boys operated by the Rev. Eleazar Wheelock. He suggested that it would be well if Samson Occum, a talented young Indian preacher, could visit England on behalf of the school. Three years later this plan was put into effect, and £12,500 was received.[7] Whitefield stated at the time, "The truly noble Lord Dartmouth espouses the cause most heartily, and his Majesty is become a contributor." Dartmouth was a Calvinist and a particular friend of Whitefield's. Wheelock's School later became Dartmouth College.

Whitefield, however, had one particular purpose in mind in this trip to America. From the time of the founding of Bethesda he had planned on adding a college, and he now sought to bring that plan to fruition. While in Georgia he wrote a *Memorial* — a history of Bethesda, stating the need of a college in that Colony and the manner in which the institution that he proposed would meet that need. The governor of the Colony entirely agreed with the plan, and therefore Whitefield soon returned to England to complete arrangements and secure a charter. He arrived July 5, 1765.

But in England, since the proposal had a religious relationship, Whitefield's petition was put by government officials before the Archbishop of Canterbury. The archbishop concurred with the idea of a college in Georgia, but required that it be operated as a Church of England institution. To this Whitefield would not agree, stating that Dissenters had been the largest givers, both to the Orphan House and the proposed college, and that the school must be established on an undenominational basis.[8]

Knowing, however, that the College of New Jersey (afterwards Princeton College) had secured a charter from the Colony in which it was situated, he planned on doing the same in Georgia.

During these days in England, although still virtually an invalid, Whitefield nevertheless conducted his ministry. Unfortunately, however, a hearer, Joseph Gurney, recorded eighteen of his Wednesday evening talks in shorthand and published them as "Whitefield's sermons."[9] They were rambling conversations with his own people and were faultily transcribed. When Whitefield saw a copy, he was shocked and declared it ought never to have been published. His trustees asserted, "These sermons are not Mr Whitefield's either in sentiment or expression."

But the *Eighteen Sermons*, being inexpensive, had several printings throughout the following century and provided the only concept of his preaching available to a great many people. They were later included in the widely-circulated volume *Seventy Five Sermons by the Rev George Whitefield*, and therefore they further falsified the public's image of his ministry.

At this time (1768) Whitefield opened three of Lady Huntingdon's chapels and also the college for young ministers that she established at Trevecca in Wales. He frequently preached again to the several nobility in her drawing room and stated, "Some more coronets are likely to be laid at the Redeemer's feet." Various of these titled persons, as well as several professional men, were regular worshipers at the Tottenham Court Road Chapel. And this was the labor of a man virtually too sick to preach!

During 1769 Whitefield made his seventh and final visit to America — his thirteenth crossing of the Atlantic. The voyage was long and trying, but it revived him physically.

He hastened to reach Bethesda and found "all things in great forwardness." The governor was ready to proceed with an Act of Assembly to establish the "College of Georgia," and Whitefield had had a builder construct two extensive wings that were to house it, one on each side of the Orphan House. He was extremely happy at Bethesda and undoubtedly would have liked to remain there for the rest of his days.

Notwithstanding such desires, he launched out once again to

declare the gospel. He was shown respect and even affection virtually everywhere, and he said, "People of all ranks flock as much as ever." After preaching in and around Philadelphia for five weeks, he moved on to New York, where he wrote, "During this month I have been above a five hundred miles circuit, and have been enabled to preach and travel through the heat of the day. The congregations have been very large. . . . Invitations crowd upon me from both ministers and people." The circuit took him through much of New England, and he even purposed to go on into Canada. But when he was in New Hampshire he proved too ill to continue and therefore reluctantly turned southward. He was drawing near to the close of his service for Christ on earth.

On September 29, on his way to Boston, he reached the town of Exeter. He intended to pass through, but found a great number of people had gathered and were insistent that he stay and preach. A platform had been prepared in a field, and as he approached it an elderly gentleman said, "Sir, you are more fit to go to bed than to preach." "True, Sir," replied Whitefield, and turning aside and looking up he stated,

Lord Jesus, I am weary in thy work, but not weary of it. If I have not yet finished my course, let me go and speak for thee once more in the fields, seal thy truth, and come home and die.[10]

Another gentleman wrote,

Mr Whitefield rose and stood erect, and his appearance alone was a powerful sermon. He remained several minutes unable to speak, and then said, 'I will wait for the gracious assistance of God. . . .'

He then delivered, perhaps, one of his best sermons. 'I go,' he cried, 'I go to a rest prepared; my sun has arisen and by aid from Heaven has given light to many. It is now about to set — no, it is about to rise to the zenith of eternal glory. Many may outlive me on earth, but they cannot outlive me in Heaven.

'Oh thought divine! I shall soon be in a world where time, age, pain and sorrow are unknown. My body fails, my spirit expands. How willingly would I live to preach Christ! But I die to be with Him!'[11]

Whitefield's sermon was from the Scripture, "Examine yourselves, whether ye be in the faith." It was two hours in length and "was delivered with such clearness, pathos and eloquence" that many hearers stated it was the greatest sermon they ever heard from him.[12]

Following this tremendous effort, Whitefield went on to the home of the Rev. Jonathan Parsons, of the Old South Presbyterian Church in Newburyport. While the family was at supper, he said he was tired and would go to bed. He was on a landing on the stairs when the door was opened to admit a host who had gathered outside and they earnestly requested that he preach. He paused, candle in hand, and preached Christ till the candle burned out in its socket and died away. That candle was symbolic of his life, which was also burned out and speedily dying away.

Richard Smith, a young man who traveled with him, reported that Whitefield awoke about 2 in the morning and seemed to pant for breath. "A good pulpit sweat to-day," he said, "may give me relief; I shall be better after preaching." Smith told him he wished he would not preach so often, but Whitefield answered, "I had rather wear out than rust out."

He woke again at 4. He got out of bed and opened the window, saying, "I am almost suffocated, I can scarce breathe." Mr. Parsons came in, and Smith went to bring the doctor. "On my coming back," he stated, "I saw death on his face. His eyes were fixed, his under-lip drawing inward every time he drew breath. . . ."

At 7 that morning, Sunday, September 30, 1770, George Whitefield ceased all struggle on earth, and his soul took its flight to the presence of God. He entered the land for which he had been prepared by divine grace, the land for which he had longed and to which he had directed countless numbers of mankind. To the sorrow of thousands he was indeed "absent from the body," but to the inestimable delight of the Hosts of Heaven he was welcomed to be with Christ, which is far, far better. Of him Bunyan's oft-quoted words may well be used: "And all the trumpets sounded for him on the other side."

(When the present author is stirring at 7 in the morning, he frequently reminds himself that Whitefield had been active since 4. Arising at that early time, he spent the first hour in communion with God, reading and praying over a portion of the Scriptures, praising God and also interceding with Him for lost souls in general and for several in particular.

At 5 he preached, and virtually always to a host of men and women. John Newton, the converted slavetrader, stated, "I have seen Moorfields as full of torches at 5 in the morning as the Haymarket is on a theatre night." And by 7 Whitefield had often set out on an evangelistic journey or was writing letters or meeting the first of the number who came seeking spiritual advice.)

23

Whitefield Remembered

O n Tuesday, October 2, tears flowed irrepressibly as the
funeral service of the incomparable evangelist was conducted
in the First Presbyterian Church of Newburyport,
Massachusetts. The service was one of natural sorrow and yet of
Christian triumph as believers again experienced the certainty that
George Whitefield was "present with the Lord."

Whitefield had assured Trustee Keen that if he died abroad, he
wanted the official service in England to be conducted by John
Wesley. Accordingly, Wesley preached first in the Chapel and then in
the Tabernacle, paying affectionate tribute to his associate's qualities
and accomplishments. He mentioned especially Whitefield's active
ministry, his tenderheartedness, charitableness, friendliness, purity,
and courage. He concluded with the statement, "Have we read or
heard of any person, who called so many thousands, so many myriads
of sinners to repentance." And numerous tributes to his abilities, his
zeal, and his preeminent winning of souls were spoken or written by
various friends around the world.

Charles Wesley, undoubtedly the man who knew him best, wrote
An Elegy on the Late Rev George Whitefield, M.A., 536 lines in
length. Even during the period of their separation, Charles had been
influenced by Whitefield's forgiving nature and innate friendship, and
it was these qualities, together with his relentless labor and transcendent preaching, which Wesley enlarged throughout his poetic tribute.
We have already seen several of its lines, and now we notice the following further passage:

> *Lover of all mankind, his life he gave,*
> *Christ to exalt, and precious souls to save:*

> *Nor age nor sickness could abate his zeal*
> > *To feed the flock, and serve the Master's will,*
> *Though spent with pain, and toils that never ceased,*
> > *He laboured on, nor asked to be released:*
> *Though daily waiting for the welcome word,*
> > *Longing to be dissolved and meet his Lord,*
> *Yet still he strangely lived, by means unknown,*
> > *In deaths immortal till his work was done,*
> *And wished for Christ his latest breath to spend,*
> > *That life and labour might together end.*[1]

William Cowper, who was a contemporary of Whitefield, in his poem "Hope" described the hostility he had long borne from the world, and then remarked,

> *He loved the world that hated him: the tear*
> > *That dropped upon his Bible was sincere;*
> *Assailed by scandal and the tongue of strife,*
> > *His only answer was a blameless life,*
> *And he that forged and he that threw the dart,*
> > *Had each a brother's interest in his heart.*[2]

The Rev. Henry Venn left a statement as to the immensity of Whitefield's labors: "One cannot but stand amazed that his mortal frame could, for the space of thirty years, sustain the weight of them. . . . Who would think it possible that a person . . . should speak in the compass of a single week (and that for years) in general forty hours, and in very many weeks, sixty, and that to thousands; and after this labour, instead of taking any rest, should be offering up prayers and intercessions, with hymns and spiritual songs, as his manner was, in every house to which he was invited."[3]

Sir James Stephen said, "If the time spent in travelling from place to place and some brief intervals of repose and preparation be subtracted, his whole life may be said to have been consumed in the delivery of one continuous or scarcely interrupted sermon."[4]

Moreover, it is evident that Whitefield's congregations, both in the individual instances and as to the totality of his lifetime (in those days before the electrical amplification of sound), were the largest ever reached by the human voice in the history of mankind.

We notice also the breadth of his appeal. He had the hearing of the coal miners of Kingswood and the slaves of America, and they understood his message. John Foster states that his preaching ". . . had the effect of giving his ideas a distinct and matchlessly vivid enouncement; insomuch that ignorant and half-barbarous men, seemed in a way that amazed even themselves, to understand Christian truths on their first delivery."[5] He was equally understood by children as by adults, and Howell Harris tells of going "To hear Bro Whitefield preach to little children, many hundreds of them, in their own infant language."

Yet he also preached with full effect, as we have seen, to the learned and sophisticated nobility of England. We have but to recall the tributes paid by such ones as the Duchess of Marlborough, the Earl of Chesterfield, Lord Bolingbroke, David Hume, and numerous others in England. And likewise we think of Benjamin Franklin, Governor Belcher, and Jonathan Edwards as indicating the intellectual strength of those who heard him with profit in America.

Whitefield also held to an exceptionally steady course, moving neither to the right hand nor to the left from the first to the last. Bishop Ryle points out that this was true concerning his doctrinal convictions. "Whitefield never turned again to asceticism, legalism, mysticism or strange views of Christian Perfection. . . . Of all the little band of Oxford Methodists, none seems to have got hold so soon of clear views of Christ's gospel and none kept them so unwaveringly to the end."[6]

This was also true of the overall purpose of his life. Isaac Taylor, a writer who invariably expressed himself with great carefulness, declared, "It would not be easy to name an instance, surpassing that of Whitefield, of a thorough uniformity of conduct and intention, held to from the moment of a man's coming before the world, to the very last hour of his life."

But what were Whitefield's faults? During his early twenties he placed too much emphasis on impressions rather than on the clear statements of Scripture. Likewise, he too easily accepted the criticisms made against certain ministers and repeated them. These tendencies, however, he soon overcame. His chief fault was his condoning the practice of slavery, the one dark blot on his otherwise spotless record.

Indeed, George Whitefield was a holy man. When Christians think of lives eminent for holiness, they usually recall such men as David Brainerd, Robert Murray McCheyne, and Henry Martyn. But Whitefield fully deserves a place among these men of God. The fruit of the Spirit — "love, joy, peace, long-suffering, gentleness, goodness, faith, meekness, temperance" — was abundantly characteristic of his life. He not only spent the hour from 4 till 5 in the morning in communion with God, but he lived in the spirit of prayer throughout the day, and prayer proved indeed his "native air."

We must also inquire, What were Whitefield's accomplishments? Throughout his lifetime and for several years after his death he was known as "the leader and founder of Methodism." Yet, as we have seen, he willingly relinquished his position as the head of the Calvinistic branch of the movement and served thereafter as "simply the servant of all."

Whitefield also taught the evangelical world a new manner of preaching. In a day when ministers in general were lacking in zeal and were apologetic in preaching, he preached the gospel with aggressive zeal and undaunted courage. He set mankind on fire wherever he went, and numerous men, learning from his example, began to preach after the same manner. For a hundred years his style of direct application was practiced in the overwhelming majority of Protestant pulpits.

He likewise held to the fundamentals of the faith. He believed in the inerrancy of the Bible, the Deity, virgin birth, atoning death, and literal resurrection of Jesus Christ, and that salvation is not by works but by grace. These truths he declared so consistently that they gradually filtered into a vast multitude of consciences, and for at least a century after his death they were preached in the greater number of churches in both Britain and America.

Of course, John and Charles Wesley, Lady Huntingdon, Howell Harris, John Cennick, and numerous others gave their full strength in the religious revival that then transformed the English-speaking world. It was a work of which J. R. Green stated,

> . . . a religious revival burst forth . . . which changed in a few years the whole temper of English society. The Church was restored to life and activity. Religion carried to the hearts of the people a fresh spirit of moral zeal, while it purified our literature and our manners. A new philanthropy reformed our prisons, infused clemency and wisdom into our

penal laws, abolished the slave trade, and gave the first impulse to popular education.[7]

But as Bishop Ryle says, "Whitefield was entirely chief and first among the English Reformers of the 18th century." He initiated almost all of its enterprises — the open-air preaching, the use of lay preachers, the publishing of a magazine, the organizing of an association, and the holding of a conference. And by his thirteen crossings of the ocean, he provided the international scope of the movement. Among his accomplishments there must be recognized the host of men and women he led to Jesus Christ and the large part he played in this great work of revival on both sides of the Atlantic.

John Greenleaf Whittier, the American Quaker poet, lived not far from Newburyport, Massachusetts. He commemorated Whitefield in his poem "The Preacher," in which he says,

> Under the church in Federal Street,
>   Under the tread of its Sabbath feet,
> Walled about by its basement stones,
>   Lie the marvellous preacher's bones.
> Long shall the traveller strain his eye
>   From the railroad car as it passes by,
> And the vanishing town behind him search
>   For the slender spire of the Whitefield Church,
> And feel for one moment the ghosts of trade,
>   And fashion and folly and pleasure laid,
> By the thought of that life of pure intent,
>   That voice of warning yet eloquent,
> Of one on the errands of angels sent.
>   And if, where he laboured, the flood of sin,
> Like a tide from the harbour bar sets in,
>   And over a life of time and sense,
> The church spires lift their vain defence . . .
>   Still, as the gem in its civic crown,
> Precious beyond the world's renown,
>   His memory hallows that ancient town.[8]

Notes

CHAPTER ONE
Born and Born Again
1. Arnold Dallimore, *George Whitefield: The Life and Times of the Great Evangelist of the 18th Century Revival*, Volume 1 (Edinburgh: Banner of Truth; Westchester, IL: Crossway Books), pp. 43, 44.
2. *Ibid.*, p. 46; *George Whitefield's Journals* (Edinburgh: Banner of Truth, 1960), pp. 37, 38. Hereafter referred to as *Journals*.
3. See Paternal Pedigree Chart, *Whitefield: Life and Times*, p. 39.
4. *Ibid.*, p. 56.
5. *Ibid.*, p. 64.
6. "An Elegy on the Late Reverend George Whitefield," *The Journal of Charles Wesley*, Volume 2 (Grand Rapids, MI: Baker, n.d.), p. 419.
7. *Whitefield: Life and Times*, p. 68.
8. *Ibid.*, p. 73; sermon "All Men's Place" in *Sermons on Important Subjects*, the Reverend G. Whitefield (London: Baynes, 1825), p. 702.
9. *Whitefield: Life and Times*, p. 74.
10. *Ibid.*, p. 76.

CHAPTER TWO
Preaching That Startled the Nation
1. *Whitefield: Life and Times*, p. 81.
2. *Ibid.*
3. *Ibid.*,p. 85; "Elegy," lines 121-129.
4. *Ibid.*, pp. 86, 87; sermon "The Good Shepherd," *Sermons on Important Subjects*, p. 733.
5. *A Diary of George Whitefield* (unpublished), the British Museum, Manuscripts Division, entry May 16, 1736.
6. *The Works of the Reverend George Whitefield* (Edinburgh and London: Dilly, 1771), pp. 18, 19.
7. *Diary*, May 18, 1736.
8. *Whitefield: Life and Times*, p. 110.
9. *Journal*, pp. 110, 111.
10. *Whitefield: Life and Times*, p. 114.
11. *The Life and Times of the Countess of Huntingdon*, Volume 1 (London, 1840), p. 20.

12. *Ibid.*, p. 25.
13. *Whitefield: Life and Times*, p. 133.
14. *Ibid.*, p. 139.

CHAPTER THREE
Missionary to Georgia
1. *The Journal of the Reverend John Wesley*, Volume 1 (London: Epworth Press, 1938), p. 138.
2. *Whitefield: Life and Times*, p. 151.
3. *Ibid.*
4. *Collections of the Georgia Historical Society*, "The Journal of Secretary Stephens," Supplement to Volume 4, June 4 – July 2. Also *Whitefield: Life and Times*, p. 203.

CHAPTER FOUR
Into the Open Air
1. William Holland, *A Narrative of the Work of the Lord in England*, (London: Moravian Church Library, Muswell Hill). Also cited in *John Wesley's Journal*, Volume 1, p. 476. Also in *Whitefield: Life and Times*, p. 183.
2. *John Wesley's Journal*, Volume 1, p. 476.
3. *Whitefield: Life and Times*, pp. 194, 195.
4. *Ibid.*, p. 221.
5. *Ibid.*
6. *Ibid.*, p. 220.
7. *Ibid.*, p. 229.
8. *Ibid.*, p. 240.
9. George J. Stevenson, *Memorials of the Wesley Family* (London, 1876), p. 216.
10. *Whitefield: Life and Times*, p. 256.
11. *Ibid.*, p. 263.
12. *Ibid.*, pp. 263, 264.
13. *John Wesley's Journal*, Volume 2, p. 167.
14. *Ibid.*, p. 201.

CHAPTER FIVE
Into the Open Air in London
1. John Gillies, *Memoirs of the Life of the Reverend George Whitefield* (London and Edinburgh: Dilly, 1772), p. 42; *Whitefield:Life and Times*, pp. 287, 288.
2. *Ibid.*, p. 289.
3. *Ibid.*, pp. 289-291.
4. *Ibid.*, pp. 292, 293.
5. Luke Tyerman, *Life of the Rev George Whitefield*, Volume 1 (London: Hodder and Stoughton, 1877), p. 217.
6. John Foster, *Critical Essays* (London: Bohn, 1856), p. 70.
7. *Whitefield: Life and Times*, p. 294.
8. *Ibid.*, p. 372.
9. *Ibid.*
10. *Ibid.*, pp. 372, 373.
11. *Ibid.*, p. 373.

12. *Ibid.*, p. 374.
13. *Ibid.*, pp. 376, 377.
14. *Ibid.*, pp. 373, 374.

CHAPTER SIX
Doctrinal Differences and Sad Divisions
1. *John Wesley's Letters*, Volume 1, p. 302.
2. Robert Southey, *Life of Wesley*, Volume 2 (London: Longmans, 1858), p. 208.
3. Sermon "Free Grace," found in various editions of *Wesley's Works*, and in *Sermons on Several Occasions by the Rev John Wesley, M.A.*, Volume 3 (London: Mason, 1847), p. 359; *Whitefield: Life and Times*, pp. 310-313.
4. *Ibid.*, p. 315.
5. *Ibid.*
6. *Ibid*, pp. 316, 317. Also John Wesley, *A Plain Account of Christian Perfection* (London: Epworth, n.d.), pp. 15, 16.

CHAPTER SEVEN
Doctrinal Convictions
1. *Whitefield: Life and Times*, Volume 1, p. 398.
2. *Ibid.*, pp. 399, 400.
3. Whitefield's *Works*, Volume 1, p. 67.
4. *Ibid.*, p. 66.
5. *Whitefield: Life and Times*, p. 404.
6. *Ibid.*, p. 406.
7. *Ibid.*
8. *Ibid.*, p. 407.
9. *Ibid.*, pp. 407, 408.
10. *Ibid.*, p. 408.

CHAPTER EIGHT
The House of Mercy
1. *Whitefield: Life and Times*, Volume 1, p. 433.
2. *Ibid.*, p. 468.
3. *Ibid.*, p. 472.
4. *Ibid.*, p. 439.
5. *Ibid.*, pp. 481, 482.
6. *Ibid.*, pp. 491, 492.
7. *Ibid.*, p. 496.
8. *Ibid.*, p. 506.

CHAPTER NINE
Laboring in the Great Awakening
1. *Whitefield: Life and Times*, Volume 1, pp. 511, 512.
2. *Ibid.*, p. 513.
3. *Ibid.*
4. *Ibid.*, p. 517.
5. Tyerman's *Whitefield*, Volume 1, p. 400.
6. Stated by Wesley's friend, John Whitehead, in his *The Life of John Wesley, M.A. and The Life of Charles Wesley, M.A.* (New York: Worthington, n.d.), p. 359.

7. Thomas Prince, *Christian History*, Volume for 1744, pp. 379, 386; *Whitefield: Life and Times*, pp. 534, 535.
8. Iain H. Murray, *Jonathan Edwards: A New Biography* (Edinburgh: The Banner of Truth, 1987), pp. 157, 158.
9. *Whitefield: Life and Times*, p. 537.
10. *Ibid.*, p. 538.
11. *Ibid.*, p. 539.
12. *The Spiritual Travels of Nathan Cole.* See Leonard W. Larabee, in the *William and Mary Quarterly*, 3rd series, VII, 1950, pp. 589, 590. Also *Whitefield: Life and Times*, p. 541.
13. J. B. Wakely, *Anecdotes of the Rev George Whitefield* (London: Hodder, 1900), pp. 344, 347.
14. *Whitefield: Life and Times*, p. 575.
15. *Ibid.*, p. 577.

CHAPTER TEN
Whitefield's Darkest Hour
1. *Whitefield: Life and Times*, Volume 2, p. 45.
2. *Ibid.*, p. 46.
3. *Ibid.*, p. 44.
4. *An Letter to the Rev Mr John Wesley in Answer to His Sermon Entitled "Free Grace"; Whitefield: Life and Times*, Volume 2, p. 552.
5. Introduction to Sermon "Free Grace," found in any issue of Wesley's *Works*; *Whitefield: Life and Times*, Volume 2, p. 56.
6. *Ibid.*, pp. 71-73.
7. *Ibid.*, pp. 76, 77.
8. Whitefield's *Works*, Volume 2, p. 466; *Whitefield: Life and Times*, Volume 2, p. 77.

CHAPTER ELEVEN
Scotland
1. *Whitefield: Life and Times*, Volume 2, p. 86.
2. *Ibid.*, pp. 86, 87.
3. *Ibid.*, p. 88.
4. *Ibid.*, p. 90.
5. *Ibid.*, p. 93.
6. *Ibid.*, p. 95.
7. *Ibid.*, p. 91.
8. *Ibid.*, p. 96.
9. *Ibid.*, pp. 97, 98.

CHAPTER TWELVE
Marriage
1. *Whitefield: Life and Times*, Volume 2, p. 106.
2. *Ibid.*, p. 107.
3. *Ibid.*, p. 108.
4. *Ibid.*, p. 109.
5. *Ibid.*, p. 110.
6. *Ibid.*, p. 168.

CHAPTER THIRTEEN
The Revival at Cambuslang
1. *Whitefield: Life and Times*, Volume 2, pp. 122, 123.
2. *Ibid.*, p. 123.
3. *Ibid.*, pp. 124, 125.
4. *Ibid.*, p. 125.
5. *Ibid.*, p. 126.
6. *Ibid.*, pp. 129, 130.
7. *Ibid.*, p. 131.
8. *Ibid.*, pp. 136, 137.

CHAPTER FOURTEEN
The First Organizing of Methodism
1. *Selected Trevecca Letters*, 1742-1747, Transcribed and Annotated by Gomer Morgan Roberts, M.A. (Caernarvon: The Calvinistic Methodist Bookroom, 1956), p. 40.
2. *Two Calvinistic Methodist Chapels, 1743-1811*, "The London Tabernacle and the Spa Fields Chapel," ed. Edwin Welch (London: London Records Society, 1975), pp. 14, 15.
3. *The Tabernacle Minutes*.
4. *Ibid.*, p. 18.
5. Tyerman's *Whitefield*, Volume 2, p. 287.
6. *Whitefield: Life and Times*, p. 156.

CHAPTER FIFTEEN
Meeting the Mob
1. *Whitefield: Life and Times*, Volume 2, p. 161; Hugh J. Hughes, *Life of Howell Harris* (London, 1892), pp. 142, 143.
2. *Whitefield: Life and Times*, p. 162; *Howell Harris, Reformer and Soldier*, ed. Rev. Tom Beynon (Caernarvon: Calvinistic Methodist Historical Society, 1958), p. 35.
3. Cennick's manuscript *Memorable Passages Relating to the Awakening in Wiltshire* (unpublished), entry of June 23, 1741.
4. *John Wesley's Journal*, Volume 3, pp. 99, 100.
5. *Charles Wesley's Journal*, Volume 1, pp. 324, 325.
6. *Whitefield: Life and Times*, Volume 2, pp. 165, 166.
7. Tyerman's *Whitefield*, Volume 2, p. 115.
8. *Whitefield: Life and Times*, Volume 2, p. 174.

CHAPTER SIXTEEN
Healing the Wounds and Completing the Work in America
1. *Whitefield: Life and Times*, Volume 2, p. 180; *Christian History*, 1744, pp. 395-397.
2. *Whitefield: Life and Times*, Volume 2, p. 181; Joseph Tracy, *The Great Awakening*, pp. 136-142.
3. *Whitefield: Life and Times*, p. 195.
4. *Ibid.*, p. 212.
5. *Ibid.*, p. 233.
6. *Ibid.*, p. 220.

CHAPTER SEVENTEEN
"Let the Name of Whitefield Perish"
1. Whitefield: Life and Times, Volume 2, p. 249.
2. Ibid., pp. 250, 251.
3. Ibid., pp. 257, 258.

CHAPTER EIGHTEEN
The Gospel to the Aristocracy in England
1. Tyerman's Whitefield, Volume 2, pp. 209, 210; Whitefield: Life and Times, Volume 2, pp. 265, 266.
2. Whitefield: Life and Times, p. 269; Life and Times of Selina, Countess of Huntingdon, Volume 1 (London, 1840), p. 179.
3. Whitefield: Life and Times, p. 269.
4. Ibid., p. 270.
5. Ibid., p. 271.
6. Ibid., p. 274.
7. Life and Times of Selina, Countess of Huntingdon, Volume 1, p. 225; Whitefield: Life and Times, pp. 277, 278.

CHAPTER NINETEEN
"Let Me Be But the Servant of All"
1. Whitefield: Life and Times, Volume 2, p. 336; John Wesley's Journal, Volume 3, p. 440.
2. Ibid., p. 439.
3. Whitefield, Works, Volume 3, pp. 44, 45; Whitefield: Life and Times, p. 347.
4. Ibid., p. 352.
5. Ibid.
6. Gillies, Memoirs of the Life of Whitefield, pp. 224, 225.
7. Tyerman's Whitefield, Volume 2, p. 475.

CHAPTER TWENTY
Associates
1. John Wesley's Journal, Volume III, p. 96.
2. Whitefield: Life and Times, Volume 2, p. 344.
3. Ibid., p. 375.
4. Ibid., pp. 377, 378; J. E. Hutton, John Cennick. A Sketch (Moravian Publication Office, n.d.), pp. 59, 60.
5. Whitefield: Life and Times, p. 379.
6. Ibid., p. 296.
7. Ibid.
8. Ibid., p. 298.
9. Ibid., p. 300.
10. The Papers of Benjamin Franklin, Volume 3, ed. Leonard W. Larabee (New Haven, CT: Yale University Press, 1959), p. 169; Whitefield: Life and Times, p. 442.
11. Ibid. (both sources).
12. Ibid., p. 443.
13. Ibid.
14. Ibid., p. 444.
15. Ibid., p. 445.

16. *Ibid.*, p. 448.
17. *Ibid.*, p. 453.

CHAPTER TWENTY-ONE
Building for God
1. *Whitefield: Life and Times*, Volume 2, p. 354.
2. *Life and Times of the Countess of Huntingdon*, Volume 2, p. 379; *Whitefield: Life and Times*, Volume 2, p. 358.
3. *Ibid.*, p. 359.
4. *Ibid.*, p. 387.
5. *Ibid.*

CHAPTER TWENTY-TWO
"Weary in Thy Work, But Not Weary of It"
1. Gillies, *Memoirs of Whitefield*, p. 226.
2. *Ibid.*, p. 231.
3. *Whitefield: Life and Times*, Volume 2, pp. 407-409.
4. *Ibid.*, p. 407.
5. *Ibid.*, p. 419.
6. *Ibid.*, p. 420.
7. *Ibid.*, pp. 459, 460.
8. *Ibid.*, pp. 456, 457.
9. *Eighteen Sermons, by the Rev George Whitefield*, "Recorded and Transposed by Joseph Gurney" (London, 1770).
10. *Memoirs of Whitefield*, p. 270.
11. Joseph Belcher, *A Biography of George Whitefield* (New York, 1857), p. 455.
12. Gillies, *Memoirs of Whitefield*, pp. 271-274; *Whitefield: Life and Times*, pp. 504-506.

CHAPTER TWENTY-THREE
Whitefield Remembered
1. *The Journal of the Rev Charles Wesley, M.A.*, Volume 2 (Grand Rapids, MI: Baker, 1980), pp. 418-431, lines 445-456.
2. William Cowper, "Hope," Tyerman's *Whitefield*, Volume 2, p. 613.
3. Gillies, *Memoirs of Whitefield*, pp. 362, 363; *Whitefield: Life and Times*, p. 521.
4. Stephen, Sir James, *Essays in Ecclesiastical Biography* (London: Longmans, 1883), pp. 384, 385; *Whitefield: Life and Times*, p. 522.
5. John Foster, *Critical Essays*, Volume 2 (London: Bohn, 1865), p. 67.
6. J.C. Ryle, *Christian Leaders of the Eighteenth Century* (Edinburgh: Banner of Truth, 1978).
7. J. R. Green, *A Short History of the English People* (Harper ed., 1899), pp. 736, 737.
8. John Greenleaf Whittier, "The Preacher," *Complete Poetical Works* (Boston: Houghton Mifflin, 1882), p. 254.

Select Bibliography

Primary

Anonymous, *Sketches of Life and Labours of the Rev George Whitefield with Two Discourses of 1739.* Johnstone, Edinburgh, and London: n.d.

Beynon, Tom, ed., *Howell Harris, Reformer and Soldier.* Caernarvon: Calvinistic Methodist Bookroom, 1958.

——, ed., *Howell Harris's Visits to London.* Aberstwyth: Cambrian News Press, 1960.

——, ed., *Howell Harris's Visits to Pembrokeshire.* Aberstwyth: Cambrian News Press, 1966.

Cennick, John, *Village Discourses, with a Life of Cennick by Matthew Wilks.* London: Sherwood, 1819. 2 vols.

Clarke, Samuel, *Annotations on the Bible: With a Recommendatory Preface by George Whitefield.* London: 1759.

Davies, Samuel, *The Reverend Samuel Davies Abroad. The Diary of a Journey to England and Scotland.* Edited and with an introduction by George William Pilcher. Urbana, Chicago, London: University of Illinois Press, 1967.

Doddridge, Philip, *The Life of Colonel James Gardiner.* London: 1747.

Edwards, Jonathan. *The Works of Jonathan Edwards*, with memoir by Sereno E. Dwight. Bungay: 1834. 2 vols. (Reprinted by Edinburgh: Banner of Truth, 1974.)

Franklin, Benjamin, *The Papers of Benjamin Franklin*, edited by Leonard W. Larabee. New Haven, CT: Yale University Press, 1959. 9 vols.

Gillies, John, *Memoirs of the Life of the Rev George Whitefield, M.A.* London: E. & C. Dilly, 1772. 2nd edition revised and corrected by Aaron C. Seymour, Dublin: 1811. An 1838 edition Hartford, Connecticut, "with large additions and improvements."

——, *Historical Collections Relating to Remarkable Periods of the Success of the Gospel and Eminent Instruments Employed in Promoting It, II.* Glasgow: 1743.

Habersham, James, *The Letters of James Habersham, 1756-1775.*

Savannah: The Collections of the Georgia Historical Society, 1904, Volume VI.

Harvard College, *The Testimony of the President, Professors, Tutors, and Hebrew Instructor of Harvard College Against the Rev Mr George Whitefield and His Conduct*. Boston: T. Fleet, 1744. 15 pp.

Heimert, Allan and Miller, Perry, eds., *The Great Awakening: Documents Illustrating the Crisis and Its Consequences*. Indianapolis and New York: Bobbs-Merrill, 1967.

Jones, M. H., *The Trevecka Letters*. Caernarvon: Calvinistic Methodist Bookroom, 1932.

Prince, Thomas, Jr., ed., *The Christian History, Containing Accounts of the Revival and Propagation of Religion in Great Britain and America. For the Year 1743*. Boston: 1744.

___ , ed., *The Christian History, Containing Accounts of the Revival and Propagation of Religion in Great Britain and America. For the Year 1744*. Boston: 1745.

Roberts, Gomer Morgan, ed., *Selected Trevecka Letters, 1742-1747*. Caernarvon: Calvinistic Methodist Bookroom, 1956.

___ , *Selected Trevecka Letters, 1747-1794*. Caernarvon: Calvinistic Methodist Bookroom, 1962.

Robe, James, *The Revival of Religion at Kilsyth, Cambuslang and Other Places in 1742*. Glasgow: William Collins, 1840.

Scougal, Henry, *The Life of God in the Soul of Man*, first published 1677, reprinted Philadelphia: Westminster, n.d.

Smith, Josiah, *The Character, Preaching &c. of the Rev Mr George Whitefield, Impartially Presented and Supported, in a Sermon, Preached in Charleston, South Carolina March 26, 1740*. Boston: 1740. Reprinted as introduction to *Sermons on Important Subjects by the Rev G. Whitefield*. London: 1825; name of author erroneously given as "Joseph Smith."

Wesley, Charles, *The Journal of Charles Wesley*. London: Wesleyan Methodist Bookroom, n.d. 2 vols. "An Elegy on the Late Rev George Whitefield, M.A." in Volume 2, pp. 418-431.

Wesley, John, *The Journal of John Wesley*. Standard edition, edited by Nehemiah Curnock, bicentenary issue. London: The Epworth Press, 1938. 8 vols.

___ , *The Letters of John Wesley*. Standard edition, London: The Epworth Press, 1931. 8 vols.

___ , *The Works of John Wesley*. London: 1872, 12th edition. 14 vols.

Whitefield, George, *The Works of George Whitefield*. London and Edinburgh: 1771. 6 vols. Volumes 1, 2, and 3 contain his letters, Volume 4 his miscellaneous writings, and Volumes 5 and 6 his sermons. Volume 1 republished, with additional letters, Edinburgh: Banner of Truth, 1976.

___ , *Journals*, together with his *A Short Account of God's Dealing with George Whitefield* and *A Further Account.* Included also is *An Unpublished Journal.* Edinburgh: Banner of Truth, 1960.

___ , *Newly Discovered Letters of George Whitefield, 1745-46*, edited by John W. Christie, *Journal of the Presbyterian Historical Society*, XXXII, Nos. 2, 3 and 4, 1954.

___ , *Sermons on Important Subjects by the Rev George Whitefield, M.A.*, with memoir by Samuel Drew and dissertation by the Rev. Josiah Smith. London: 1825. Includes 75 sermons.

Secondary

Abbey, Charles J. and Overton, John H., *The English Church in the 18th Century.* London: 1878. 2 vols.

Alexander, Archibald, *The Log College*, Biographical Sketches of William Tennent and His Students. 1851. Reprinted Edinburgh: Banner of Truth, 1968.

Andrews, J. R., *George Whitefield, a Light Rising in Obscurity.* London: Morgan & Chase, 2nd edition, revised and enlarged, 1930.

Austin, Roland, *A Bibliography of the Works of George Whitefield*, Proceedings of Wesley Historical Society, Vol. X, Parts 7 and 8.

Baker, Frank, *John Cennick, A Handlist of His Writings*, Publication No. 5 of the Wesley Historical Society, 1958.

Balleine, G. R., *A History of the Evangelical Party in the Church of England.* London: Longmans, 1908.

Bathafarn: The Journal of the Historical Society of the Methodist Church in Wales. Issues of 1945-1955, various editors.

Belcher, Joseph, *George Whitefield, a Biography with Special Reference to His Labours in America.* New York: American Tract Society, 1857.

Belden, Albert D., *George Whitefield — The Awakener. A Modern Study of the Evangelical Revival.* London: Sampson Low, Marston, 1930.

Bennet and Bogue, *The History of the Dissenters from 1688 to 1800.* 2 vols.

Bennett, Richard, *The Early Life of Howell Harris.* First published in Welsh under title *The Dawn of Welsh Calvinistic Methodism*, 1909. Published in English, Edinburgh: Banner of Truth, 1962.

Billingsley, Amos Stevens, *The Life of the Great Preacher Rev George Whitefield, 'Prince of Pulpit Orators,'* with the Secret of His Success and Specimens of His Sermons. Philadelphia: P. W. Ziegler, 1878.

Bready, John Wesley, *England: Before and After Wesley: The Evangelical Revival and Social Reform.* London: Hodder and Stoughton, 1938.

Bull, Josiah, *John Newton*, An Autobiography and Narrative. London: The Religious Tract Society, 1868.

Butler, Dugald, *John Wesley and George Whitefield in Scotland, or the Influence of the Oxford Methodists on Scottish Religion.* Edinburgh and London: Wm. Blackwood, 1898.

Couillard, Vernon Williams, *The Theology of John Cennick*. Nazareth, PA: The Moravian Historical Society, 1957.

Coke, Thomas and Moore, Henry, *The Life of the Reverend John Wesley*. London: Milner, 1792.

Dargan, Edwin C., *A History of Preaching*, Volume 1: *A.D. 70-1572*, Volume 2: *1572-1900*. First published 1904, reprinted Grand Rapids, MI: Baker, 1954, 2 vols. in 1.

Dearnley, I. H., *An Official Guide to Kingswood and Hanham*. Cheltenham and London: J. Burrow & Co., n.d.

Eayrs, George, *Wesley, Kingswood and Its Free Churches*. London: Simpkin, Marshall, 1911.

____, *Wesley: Christian Philosopher and Church Founder*. London: Epworth, 1926.

Edwards, Maldwyn, *Family Circle: A Study of the Epworth Household in Relation to John and Charles Wesley*. London: Epworth, 1946.

Fawcett, Arthur, *The Cambuslang Revival*. Edinburgh: Banner of Truth, 1971.

Fitchett, W. H., *Wesley and His Century*. Toronto: 1906.

Flint, Charles Wesley, *Charles Wesley and His Colleagues*. Washington: Public Affairs Press.

Foote, W. H., *Annals of Virginia*. First series, 1850. Reprinted Richmond, VA: John Knox Press, 1966.

Foster, John, *Critical Essays*. London: Bohn, 1856. 2 vols.

Gaustad, Edwin Scott, *The Great Awakening*. New York: Harper, 1957.

Gewehr, Wesley M., *The Great Awakening in Virginia, 1740-1790*. Durham, NC: Duke University Press, 1930.

Gladstone, James Paterson, *The Life and Travels of George Whitefield, M.A.* London: Longmans, Green, 1871.

Green, Richard, *The Works of John and Charles Wesley. A Biography*. London: Chas. H. Kelly, 1896.

Green, V. H., *The Young Mr. Wesley*, A Study of John Wesley and Oxford. London: Edwin Arnold, 1961.

Hardy, Edwin Noah, *George Whitefield, the Matchless Soul-winner*. New York: American Tract Society, 1938.

Hughes, J., *A Memoir of Daniel Rowland*, in Welsh Reformer Series. London: Nisbet, 1887.

____, *The Life of Howell Harris*. London: Nisbet, 1892.

Hutton, J. E., *A History of the Moravian Church*. London: Moravian Publication Office, 1909.

____, *John Cennick: A Sketch*. London: Moravian Publication Office, n.d.

Hyett, Sir F. A. and Austin, Roland, *Bibliographical Supplement to the Manual of Gloucestershire Literature*. Gloucester: 1914, pp. 505-572.

Jay, William, *Memoirs of the Life and Character of the Late Reverend Cornelius Winter*. Bath: M. Gye, 1808.

Journal of the Calvinistic Methodist Historical Society. Caernarvon: 1916-
1929. Title changed in 1930 to *Journal of the Historical Society of the
Presbyterian Church of Wales.*

Kirk, John, *The Mother of the Wesleys.* London: Jarrold and Sons, 1868.

Knight, Helen, *Lady Huntingdon and Her Friends.* New York: American
Tract Society, 1853.

Laycock, J. W., *Methodist Heroes in the Great Haworth Round. 1734-
1784.* Keighley: Rydal Press, 1909.

Loane, Marcus L., *Oxford and the Evangelical Succession.* London:
Lutterworth Press, 1950.

Lyles, Albert M., *Methodism Mocked.* London: Epworth, 1960.

Macfarlan, D., *The Revivals of the 18th Century, Particularly at
Cambuslang. With Three Sermons by the Rev George Whitefield, Taken
in Short Hand.* London and Edinburgh: John Johnstone, n.d.

MacLeane, Douglas, *A History of Pembroke College, Oxford.* Oxford:
Clarendon Press, 1897.

Maxson, Charles Hartshorn, *The Great Awakening in the Middle Colonies.*
Chicago: 1920. Reprinted Gloucester, MA: Peter Smith, 1958.

Moravian Historical Society, *The Transactions of the Moravian Historical
Society.* Nazareth, PA: Whitefield House, 1876, Volume 1, Part X.
Deals with relations between Whitefield and the Moravians at Nazareth.

New, Alfred H., *The Coronet and the Cross: Memorials of the Right Hon
Selina Countess of Huntingdon.* London: Partridge & Co., 1858.

Newton, John, *Out of the Depths, an Autobiography.* Reprinted Chicago:
Moody Press, n.d.

Ninde, E. S., *George Whitefield, Prophet-Preacher.* New York: Abingdon
Press, 1924.

Overton, John, *The Evangelical Revival in the Eighteenth Century.*
London: Longmans, Green, 1886.

Philip, Robert, *Life and Times of the Rev George Whitefield.* London:
George Virtue, 1837.

Plummer, Alfred, *The Church of England in the Eighteenth Century.*
London: Methuen Co., 1910.

Quiller-Couch, A. T., *Hetty Wesley.* London and New York: Harper Bros.,
1903.

Quincer, Sheldon B., ed., *Whitefield's Sermon Outlines. A Choice
Collection of Thirty-five Model Sermons.* Grand Rapids, MI: Eerdmans,
1956.

Rattenbury, J. Ernest, *Wesley's Legacy to the World.* London: Epworth
Press, 1928.

Roberts, Richard Owen, *A Bibliography of Evangelism and Revival.*
Unpublished manuscript.

Ryle, J. C., *Christian Leaders of the Eighteenth Century.* London: 1885;
reprinted Edinburgh: Banner of Truth, 1978.

Services at the Centenary Celebration of Whitefield's Apostolic Labours, Held in the Tabernacle, Moorfields, May 21, 1839. London: James Snow, 1839.

Seymour, A. C. H., The Life and Times of Selina, Countess of Huntingdon. By a Member of the Noble Houses of Shirley and Hastings, 2 vols. London: Sempkin, Marshall & Co. Index published by the Proceedings of the Wesley Historical Society, Volume 4, Part 8, 1906.

Simon, John S., The Revival of Religion in England in the Eighteenth Century. London: Robert Culley, n.d.

Skeats, Herbert S., The History of the Free Churches of England. London: Arthur Miall, 1868.

Southey, Robert, Life of Wesley and the Rise and Progress of Methodism. London: Longmans, 1820. New edition with notes by the late Samuel Taylor Coleridge, 1858. 2 vols.

Spurgeon, Charles Haddon, Religious Zeal Illustrated and Enforced by the Life of the Rev George Whitefield. London: The Gospel Atlas, 1885.

Stephen, Sir James, Essays in Ecclesiastical Biography. London: Longmans, 1883.

Stevenson, George J., Memorials of the Wesley Family. London: Partridge, 1876.

Stevens, Abel, History of the Methodist Episcopal Church in America. New York: Carlton & Porter, 1867. 4 vols.

Taylor, Isaac, Wesley and Methodism. New York: Harper & Bros., 1860.

Tracy, Joseph, The Great Awakening, a History of the Revival of Religion in the Time of Edwards and Whitefield. Boston: Tappan & Dennet, 1842. Reprinted Edinburgh: Banner of Truth, 1967.

Tyerman, Luke, The Life and Times of the Rev John Wesley, M.A. London: Hodder and Stoughton, 1870. 3 vols.

___ , The Oxford Methodists, Memoirs of Clayton, Ingham, Gambold, Hervey and Broughton, etc. London: Hodder and Stoughton, 1873.

___ , The Life of the Rev George Whitefield. London: Hodder and Stoughton, 1876. 2 vols.

Venn, Henry, The Life and Letters of the Rev Henry Venn, M.A. 6th edition. New York: Stanford, 1854.

Wakeley, J. B., Anecdotes of Rev George Whitefield, with a Biographical Sketch. London: Hodder and Stoughton, 1900.

Welch, Edwin, Two Calvinistic Methodist Chapels, 1743-1811. The London Tabernacle and Spa Fields Chapel. London: London Record Society, 1975.

Wicks, George Hosking, Whitefield's Legacy to Bristol and the Costwolds. Bristol: Taylor Bros., 1914.

Wood, A. Skevington, The Inextinguishable Blaze. London: The Paternoster Press, 1960.

Index